ARABO-ISLAMIC TEXTS ON
FEMALE HOMOSEXUALITY
850-1780 A.D.

Arabo-Islamic Texts on
Female Homosexuality
850-1780 A.D.

Samar Habib

\<teneo\> // press

YOUNGSTOWN, NEW YORK

Copyright 2009 Samar Habib
All rights reserved

Printed in the United States of America

ISBN: 978-1-934844-11-3

The appendix of translations and the essay "Reading the Familiarity of the Past" have been reproduced with permission from *Entertext*.

No part of this publication may be reproduced, stored in or introduced into a retrieval system, or transmitted, in any form, or by any means (electronic, mechanical, photocopying, recording, or otherwise), without the prior permission of the publisher.

Requests for permission should be directed to
permissions@teneopress.com,
or mailed to:
Teneo Press,
PO Box 349,
Youngstown, New York 14174

Acknowledgments

I'd like to thank my partner Rebecca for her encouragement and support and Aswat, the Palestinian Lesbian Organization in Haifa, which is undertaking important work in addressing homophobia in the Arab world.

The appendix of translations and the essay "Reading the Familiarity of the Past" were first published in *Entertext* 7(2), December 2007: 162-215. The author wishes to thank the editors and peer reviewers at *EnterText* for their permission to reproduce this material and for their insightful comments that led to constructive revisions of the manuscript.

The translation of "Reading the Familiarity of the Past" into Arabic and French could not have been possible without the financial support of the School of Humanities and Languages at the University of Western Sydney, Australia.

The author is also greatly indebted to the e-repository of rare Arabic manuscripts and texts, Alwaraq.net. Without this repository, access to many of the texts translated in this book would not have been possible.

Contents

A Lecture on Woman-Woman Love and
Sexuality in the Arabo-Islamic Middle East 9

Reading the Familiarity of the Past 33

Reading the Familiarity of the Past (Arabic) 47

Reading the Familiarity of the Past (French) 53

An Appendix of Texts from the Arabian Middle Ages
Concerned with Female Homosexuality 67

Endnotes 109

A Lecture on Woman-Woman Love and Sexuality in the Arabo-Islamic Middle East.[1]

First of all, I'd like to thank you for the warm welcome I have received. I find myself welcomed to a place on this earth that, I cannot deny, stirs clashing emotions within me. I feel that Palestine is always a part of my life, my imagination and political orientation. And I know also that without Palestine I may never have been born. My parents—who were children at the time of their dispossession in the 1948 diaspora—met in Lebanon and without the *Nakba* they may never have met and I might never have been born. And I add to these thoughts that I am returning to Palestine, even though I've never been here before and this is a spiritual sort of return. And it is fitting that the cause of this return is not the Church of Nativity (to which my cultural Christianity connects me) or the Temple Mount (to which my scholarly curiosity draws me) or al-Aqsa mosque (that attracts me with the promise of an old Arab-Islamic civilisation that I have come to love and admire over the years). In fact, what causes me to return to Palestine is a Palestinian Lesbian Organisation (Aswat). Palestinians and lesbians who for the first time in modern history have the capacity to found an organisation? This is certainly a place on earth I felt I must visit, even if briefly.

The existence of a Palestinian Lesbian Organisation is in itself a monumental achievement because such an organisation can facilitate networking between thinkers, intellectuals and activists from all parts of the world. Such an organisation is capable of creating dialogue and fora for discussion, and it forces ideas that contradict the status quo on its society, and it brings together scattered individuals in order to create a communal bond between them. But what I find to be the most important aspect of Aswat's work is the organisation's production and dissemination of information and literature on homosexuality in the Arabic language and collecting an archive that can be useful to Arabic-speaking lesbians in the community. This kind of organisation, in my opinion, is the most important because it allows us to educate ourselves. I sincerely hope that the impact Aswat has will be heard within Arab communities throughout the world where the misconception of homosexuality and its demonisation are the norm.

What Aswat has published in terms of literature[2] which directly and positively discusses female homosexuality in the Arab world resembles and revives an old Arab literary tradition, that can be traced back to the Abbasid dynasty of Harun al-Rashid and his son al-Ma'mun where the folktales of *A Thousand And One Nights* were collected and written down, much like al-Asfahani's almost incredible collection of song lyrics, anecdotes and tales in his encyclopaedic work *al-Aghani*. These early Arabic folklore stories never shied away from discussing the subjects of sex and sexuality candidly and mirthfully, and this is the reason why reading these texts remains a pleasurable experience in modern times. And so Aswat creates a link between this older literary canon and modern publications which allow Arab lesbians to speak about themselves and for themselves for the first time in a modern context. By publishing these writings, Aswat puts into the hands of an upcoming generation of gay and lesbian people, theories and ideas that they can use as weapons in the fight against the epistemes of patriarchal societies that seek to oppress and repress virtually everything related to sex.

It is through these writings that we can begin to emancipate ourselves from the homophobia that affects us even unconsciously through societies that reject us completely. Self-education increases our awareness and if we want to change the societies in which we live we first must attend to our own negative perceptions of ourselves. Most Arabic lesbians are suffering from a long and harsh history of oppression, and this oppression has led to the institutionalising of hiding and counterfeiting our real identities so long as we are amidst family and relatives. Most Arabic lesbians whom I have met accept leading double lives: the life of the closet around parents and relatives and a life of sexual freedom away from them. And I know that there are numerous situations and circumstances in life where declaring one's sexual orientation can be literally fatal, and most of the time we can do without such danger. Nevertheless, I cannot deny my admiration of and gratitude for the resistance that can stand in face of even this kind of imminent danger, as it so happened in New York's 1969 Stonewall riots. In 2004, on a research trip to Manhattan and Brooklyn, I spoke to Stonewall's bartender who was a young man at the time of the riots and who witnessed them first hand. He told me, that unlike some reports, the first person to physically engage the police was a butch lesbian and it was the drag queens who first came to her aid.

The kind of coming out from the closet that I am talking about comes after a difficult period involving self-education. This kind of coming out becomes an effective political strategy and it is a deliberate coming out that aims to be the living evidence of the fact that being homosexual is natural, that it is not a disease or in need of repair or annihilation. And you have within you the modest power to determine how other people are going to treat you; for if you behave like prey, they will prey on you, and if you behave as though there is something to be ashamed of or to feel guilty about, then you are reinforcing the idea that there is something calling for guilt and shame.

It is possible that I was lucky because my sexual orientation became obvious to me from an early age and I was not able to ignore it and for this reason coming out and becoming visible became necessary for my well-being. I think there is a destructive relationship between leading a double life and what one might feel about one's sexual orientation. It is possible that the next natural step for us be the move from *aswat* (voices) to *wujooh* (faces) and back. There is such tremendous power in the rhetorical act of stating, very simply, "yes I'm gay, and so what's the problem? Are you stupid?" This kind of demanding to be reckoned with shakes up a whole society that has been reared on seeing homosexuality as unnatural and a society that doesn't doubt for a moment that it is in fact wrong about this assumption.

I also know there are benefits to remaining in hiding: concealing one's sexual orientation serves a woman who does not want to lose her freedom of behaviour, a woman who wishes to obviate the clash between her and family and friends because she does not want to risk losing them. I also know that some Arab lesbians see coming out as a Western strategy and we don't have to come out in order to be free because our communities differ from those of the West. This is a popular theorem among Arab lesbians presently, but I cannot say I agree with this strategy of duality especially because the ideas that Western societies had about homosexuality were no less entrenched there, no less cruel and demonising than those we experience in Arab communities in modern times. And the means with which gay men and women achieved their civil rights and social emancipation (to an extent) was precisely through a self-affirming coming out process. This was a self-affirming process which rejected stigma and shame in order to embrace the importance of sexual fulfilment in life.

The political project of gay and lesbian activists in the West came across a great deal of vitriol from the religious right, and from the police and from the judicial system and government bodies. And these activists began to agitate for change long before the abolition of these discriminatory laws against them which permitted their countries of residence to prosecute them under state law. These oppressive laws were changed primarily because of the audacity of the few, their visibility and struggle. Gays and lesbians of the twentieth century demonstrated, and they fought with the police and they spent time in prison and were persecuted, but they had confronted their fears of being persecuted and beaten and jailed. Like the Palestinian people and their numerous *intifadas*, there comes a time when the human being rejects the imperialist control over their body and soul.

Our demands for civil rights protection under the United Nations human rights bill is not always going to be a clean and peaceful struggle. There might be a time in the future where fighting becomes inevitable, where we have to stand up for our rights, where we have to be unruly and speak with raised voices about obscene things and be prepared to lose those parts of our lives that dwell in our closet. But I don't want to make this too difficult for anyone, because by this talk I don't mean every single Arabic or Palestinian lesbian. I intend this talk for she who has already arrived at my own conclusions about visibility and coming out, she who can and wants to affect change within the community she lives, she who through her self-assertive behaviour alone is already putting into effect all the desired changes we need.

As for us Arab lesbians who live in the West, I think we have especially contributed to the problem of homophobia in our communities. We live in countries that protect our human rights but many of us still live in the closet when it comes to our communities. Ask yourself if you are capable of complete and uncompromising coming out, and whether you are capable of accepting all the losses that might accompany such a move. Ask yourself if you are able to live without the leash of concealment to which you have grown accustomed, and if you are then do so. Don't accept for your emotions to be held hostage by others, don't accept "if your mother found out, this would kill her." If you think that she is going to die because of this, then let her die. Distance yourself from anything that is injurious to your being and get away from anything that makes you doubt in your right to be as you are, and your right to be treated as a human being. Get away from anything that makes you doubt the beauty of what you are and the fact that you are outside the social norms and thank your god for being different in this way. Look for others. Educate yourself. Search and establish for yourself financial independence. Embrace your sexual urges and free yourself from the theological concept that teaches us that sex is sinful and whose penultimate goal is sacred reproduction.

Here ends my modest commentary on the condition of Arabic lesbians in general, and my commentary on the importance of coming out to our process of accepting ourselves. And we have to accept ourselves first before we ask or insist or force our presence on society through the political action of visibility and coming out. And it is not possible for every lesbian to be visible. Usually what becomes visible of gays and lesbians are the masculine women and the feminine men, because society brands them with being in contradiction to 'natural life' that is embodied in a masculine man who is active and a docile feminine woman who is acted upon. But now let us turn to the Abrahamaic religions' treatment of homosexuality. And let's start with the last of these. Many Muslims throughout the world believe that Islam and homosexuality cannot be reconciled, or if reconciled, then this is deeply flawed and sacrilegious. And it is possible for us to see any attempt at producing Islamic discourse that is accepting of homosexuality as a desperate and impossible attempt. But this is caused by an absence of a serious academic attempt to consider this matter.

I would like to share with you now my thoughts regarding an Islamic hermeneutics that can be accepting of homosexuality. First of all, I should stress that the holy Islamic texts (meaning the correct ahadith and the Quran) do not deal in a direct way with the subject of homosexuality as it appears to us in countries like Saudi Arabia or Iran or Nigeria that implement the Sharia laws where homosexuality can be dealt with punishment as severe as execution. These Islamic laws that treat homosexuality as a crime, go back to ahadith about Ali Ibn Abi Talib. After the death of the prophet, Ibn Abi Talib became, for a short period of time, the leader of the Islamic *umma*. And one day, two men who were caught having homosexual sex were brought to him. And it became apparent then that none of the prophet's companions were able to remember a hadith on how they were to punish homosexuality. It was then that Ibn Abi Talib ordered the execution of the two young men by throwing them over a rooftop and following them with rocks. And this, ladies and gentlemen, is how we arrive at the punishment of homosexuality in modern Sharia.

After this event, which was the first official punishment for homosexuality among Muslims, the religious scholars noted that the Quran did not speak with direct negativity or finality in relation to homosexuality. And thus began the project of rejecting and punishing homosexuality among some of these scholars. These scholars searched for and found some ahadith that were severed, and that claimed that the prophet had said that grinding was women fornicating with each other, and that he had also said that the doer and the done to were both to be killed in the male homosexual act.

However, in those early Islamic centuries there was no unanimous consensus among scholars and the Muslim tribes on how homosexuality was to be treated. For there were scholars who accepted homosexuality: Al-Hassan Al Bassri, for example, or Ibn Hazm, who both treated homosexuality among men candidly and positively, and they both wrote about male homosexual relations ordinarily in their writings. There was also Yahya bin Aktham in Baghdad of the ninth century. Bin Aktham was famous for his love of homosexual relations, and as the leading Islamic jurist of the state he punished fornication but found homosexuality not punishable under Islamic law.

There was also what Ibn Hazm in the 11th century AD noticed about some Muslim tribes which permitted homosexual relations while others punished it in the same manner as fornication was punished. In fact, it was Ibn Hazm himself who turned the scholars' attention to the story of Lut in the holy Quran. Ibn Hazm insists that this story was not intended to reflect punishment of homosexuality, but rather punishment for disbelief (infidelity). It is true that Lut reproaches his people for abandoning their wives and loving only other men.[3] But our scholars today insist on concluding that the story of Lot's people as it appears in the Quran is indisputable evidence of the rejection of homosexuality. And they see homosexuals across history and civilizations— homosexuals from the past, the present and the future, they see all of us as implicated in the crimes of qawm Lut. However, the story by itself and without the exegetical apparatus needed to produce homophobia cannot sustain such a mission.

There are also correct ahadith found in Sahih al-Muslim and Sahih al-Bukhari which say in a section on clothing that the prophet cursed men who behaved with the mannerisms of women and women who behaved like men, and that such people should be turned out of the Muslims' homes. This hadith itself which seems to reject gender atypical behaviour might actually have its origins in another authenticated hadith that does not quite say to turn people out of one's home. There is another hadith that speaks about an effeminate man in the home of Um Salma. In this hadith, the prophet bans the effeminate man from entering into the women's quarters as he was previously permitted to do. The reason the prophet rejected him was because he was able to give a sexualising description of one of the women to whom he was privy in her private quarters. It is obvious that the prophet turned away this man not for his gender atypical behaviours, that is, his effeminacy, but rather for his heterosexualisation of a woman to another heterosexual man. So a story about the prophet turning away one man not for his gender atypicality, but rather his sexualisation of a woman, has been turned—in another relation of the hadith—into general advice to cast out all gender atypically behaving people. If we consider the prophet's interaction with this effeminate man, his previous acceptance of him, and a rejection not based on his gender atypical behaviour, we can understand with greater awareness why the prophet never officially punished homosexuality in his lifetime.

But if there is going to be an Islamic hermeneutics that accepts homosexuality, it is still going to expect marriage and the declaration of the relationship in a public space through marriage. It is obvious that Islam does not permit any sexual relationship that is outside the marital institution. The *aya* (verse) in the Quran that discusses marital relations uses the gender neutral terms "zawjan" which means a pair, a couple, a spouse. And so a queer-friendly Islam would permit homosexual *Nikah* (marriage).

I should say that I'm speaking here from a non-religious perspective, a perspective that nourishes my scholarly curiosity. And for this reason I speak not as a Muslim, but as a humble philosopher from West Beirut and West Sydney.

As for Judaism—which armed both Christianity and Islam with the story of Sodom and Gomorrah, that forms the most common artillery in support of religion-based homophobia— some say that the Torah's telling of the story was intended to deter believers from mistreating strangers and travellers, particularly emphasising that Lot's people were intent on raping his visitor (who was an angel in disguise no less). As for the book of Leviticus which was originally intended as a book of rules and regulations for the rabbis of Leviticus, this book which states "thou shall not lie with a man as thou wouldst with a woman" also states that one is forbidden from eating shellfish and wearing garments with blended material. No one nowadays pays much attention to the forbidding of eating shellfish or wearing garments of blended cotton and say, polyester. And yet everybody still insists or mentioning the prohibition of homosexual acts between men and by extrapolation in modern times, many see that this prohibition applies to the women as well and that these prohibitions were not specific to the rabbis of Leviticus only but are commandments for one and all. But in truth, the word sodomite was not as directly connected with homosexual relations in exclusion of all other attributes of one of or pertaining to the town of Sodom. It was not until the passing of several centuries and after significant effort on the part of the religious clergy in all three monotheistic religions that the prohibition of homosexual relations became the ultimate lynchpin of interpretation on which the story of the Sodomite came to depend in modern times.

Our societies force us to choose between homosexuality and piety, but similar to John Boswell I do not see an essential disharmony between homosexuality and religiosity unless this homosexuality comes in the form of sexual behaviour that is free from the limitations set on sexual pleasure and promiscuity. And in this event, this can be the same for heterosexuals, bisexuals and homosexuals all the same.

There are other erroneous suppositions that circulate in our Arab communities and among these suppositions is the notion that homosexuality is a Western import. The truth is that homosexual relations can be found in all parts of the world and across most previous civilisations. In fact, among the Western orientalists of the 19th century, it was thought that homosexual relations were particularly rife in the Arabian desert countries. And the westerners of the time thought that homosexuality originated in the Arab Middle East and that they had imported this behaviour from us.

In this next part, I would like to show you some of the medieval Arabic writings on the subject of female homosexuality that I discovered through my research. I'd like to introduce you to the grinders (homosexual women) of the Arab civilisation as it was presented to us by male scholars of mujun, literature and science. And in order to do this in some chronological order, we should first turn to al-Hassan al-Yemeni, who died in 850 A.D. And he writes:

Grinding is an old trait in women and they find pleasure in it which facilitates the exposure of their secret and their becoming famous for it. He [i.e. Prophet Muhamad] peace be upon him (p.b.u.h) said: "women grinding each other is fornication". The first woman to set grinding was the daughter of Hassan Yamani. She came to Nu'man Bin Al-Muthir and so he took her to his wife Hind. She fell madly in love with her. Hind was the best of the folks of her time, she was completely without excesses. The daughter of Hassan did not cease to deceive her and to decorate grinding for her and to say: In the union of two women there is a pleasure that cannot be between the woman and the man. To safeguard herself from scandal and knowing that her appetite can be satisfied without accusation or fear of punishment, they had intercourse (*Ijtama'ata*). Hind found a pleasure that was even greater than the other had described and their amorous desire for each other increased – and it had never been so between women before this.

When the daughter of Hassan died, Hind sat at her grave all the time until people began to use her case for their sayings. al-Farzdak said:

I was devoted to you in a time that you bestowed kindly
Like Hind was devoted to Hassan Yamani's daughter.

al-Yemeni, as you can see, thought that Hind was smitten with the daughter of al-Hassan, and that their relationship was strong, passionate, sexual and loyal. Hind, the wife of al- Munthir (the Byzantine King) lived in the 5th century, meaning that this story takes place before the birth of Islam among the Arabs and al-Yemeni adds to this that:

> Then after them came Rughum and Najda – they romanced each other and they became famous for their grinding until Rughum's brother was taunted for his sister's behaviour. So he waited until he came upon them one day as they were having intercourse. So he killed Najda and took his sister away with him. Rughum began to incite Najda's people to kill her brother and a war erupted between them. This serves as an indication of the greatness of the pleasure they find in grinding as well as an indication of their preference for grinding over the pleasure with men.

This story shows that this particular homosexual relationship was rejected by Rughum's tribe and her brother, but the relationship was not rejected by Najda's tribe because her lover appealed to them for revenge which resulted in a war between the tribes. al-Yemeni adds to this that these grinders can be classified in two categories. "Some of them love grinding but do not hate the penis," and these women can be rescued from grinding by a man of great aptitude in pleasing women sexually.

However, al-Yemeni adds that the second category of these grinders is she who appears masculine from birth, and this becomes apparent in her from an early age. And this kind of grinder, al-Yemeni thinks, cannot be restored to the straight path. As you know, al-Yemeni's analysis doesn't really show us the reality of these Arabic homosexual women, but rather it shows us his ignorance in the matter. Western sexologists of the 1950s, with the exception of Alfred Kinsey, shared al-Yemeni's perception that homosexual women resemble men while homosexual men resembled women. Arab societies continue to hold these misconceptions today. Add to these misconceptions the notion that a feminine-acting homosexual woman is not a real homosexual, and that it is possible to convert her to heterosexuality through sex with a skilled male lover. Therefore, it is important that we read these old writings carefully, and not forget that its authors tried to place us in heteronormative sexual categories that form the status quo, in which man earns his manhood through exhibiting masculinity, and woman cannot be woman without an abundance of femininity. In the Arab world, society forces us to see an effeminate young man walking languidly as a woman.

Fortunately, the concepts that were developed in queer theory in recent decades have taught us that there is no reason to connect the sexual identity of the body with the sexual identity of the mind. And thus it became possible for us to admit our existence as individuals in more complex and nuanced ways. And now I am able to understand how it is possible to be a woman who is exceedingly feminine and also exclusively homosexual. I can also be a masculine woman in my behaviour and dress, and not be coerced into seeing this as a poor imitation of maleness. And I can also be a man without a penis, or a woman embodied within a biologically male body. And no matter what my biological sex may be, I can still refuse to be either a man or a woman, and I can feel that my sexual identity is transient, or transcendent of the social categories of man or woman.

Queer theory helps us to analyse these patriarchal texts which see that everything that is related to sex in these texts begins and ends with the man. But al-Yemeni confesses with great reluctance that for some women, sexual relations with other women are far more pleasurable than sexual relations with men. And this confession is important, and it is a confession that affirms the existence of homosexuality among women from the 9th century and even earlier. This confession shows us that Arabic homosexual women existed throughout history and civilisations. One of the funniest anecdotes related by al-Yemeni about female writers can be found in the following verses:

> A *Mutaqeeya* sketched a male slave lifting the legs of a woman he was fucking and sent it to a grinder with the following comment:
>
>> This, by your life, is my condition
>> I have naught to do with grinding
>> This shoots the hearts in an instant, like arrows
>> having a brow like darkness and a lunate
>>> countenance
>> And a figure like a cane that glows with evenness
>
>> For that is my intimacy and enticement,
>> For which I would lay down my life and fortune
>> Since this might burden you,
>> My deed does not enrich me.
>
> so the grinder sketched her a picture of a concubine grinding her and sent it to the *Mutaqeeya* and she wrote alongside it:
>
>> But my vagina succeeds and glimmers between a cheek and a freckle

> Like a dot of musk swinging above the crescent
> Revealing a pure mouth , smiling like pearls
> in which there is a savory saliva
> instantly sweet to the taste.
> And a fine neck as beautiful as the gazelle's
>
> From what I have seen of her beauty -
> And O how much have I seen! -
> I say glory to whomever moulded beauty from clay
> To create a perfect creature made of beauty.
> I came to sip from her and her extreme thirst is at a well
>
> If that is prohibited (*Haram*) then this is not lawful (*Halal*).

This final poem represents for me one of the most important and beautiful old writings on the subject. Because we hear the voice of an Arabic grinder across centuries, and yet we are still able to understand her sensations and her sufferings together. The poetess goes from describing an oral sexual act, and the thirst for sexual fulfilment at the hands of another woman, to what she says about the prohibition of satisfying one's sexual thirst and her obviously political statement that the prohibition is unlawful. This anonymous woman who allegedly addressed a guarded heterosexual woman, shows us that homosexuality is not contradictory to being Arab, but rather there is a literary and historical confluence between these two identities. And even though al-Yemeni saw that homosexuality was sinful and prohibited, he was nevertheless tolerant of their presence. And there is no incitement to violence or annihilation of these women.

As for Ahmad Ibn Yusuf Tifashi (a Muslim Arab scholar from Tunis) who died in 1253 AD, he used to treat the subject positively and he was the only scholar who stated that some "wise men" saw grinding between women as a natural desire. But I will return to Tifashi after we meet another Arabic lesbian figure from the 9th century. This woman was named Bathal and she was a freed slave who entertained at the court of the Ma'mun. What we know about this urban entertainer comes from the book *al-Aghani* by Abu Faraj al-Asfahani. The author tells us that Bathal composed more than 1,200 songs and was able to sing more than 30,000 tunes. He also tells us that Bathal was admired by many suitors who proposed to her. But she spent her life unmarried and one day:

> Al-Ma'mun was sitting with a cup in his hand when Bathal[4] began to sing the song:
>
> I see nothing more delectable than the promise
>
> But she sang it:
>
> I see nothing more delectable than grinding.
>
> Al-Ma'mun placed his cup down and turned to her and said: "Of course there is Bathal, fucking is better than grinding." So she became embarrassed and feared his wrath but he picked up his cup again and said: Finish the song and add:
>
> > I come to her when the slanderer is unaware
> > With a visit to a house empty of visitors but me
> > With a cry during the meeting and then a pause
> > And all these things are more delectable to me than dwelling [there]

Bathal arouses our curiosity in doing this. What does her audacity mean? And what is her relationship to grinding? Did she have an ongoing relationship with an anonymous female lover? Was Bathal one of those visible grinders, the masculine ones named by Al Yemeni? Or was she perhaps one of those women that made her homosexuality more difficult to detect because of hyper-femininity? I think that Bathal was homosexual, not because I want her to be this way, or because I am forcing values and epistemes from our modern times onto a previous millennium but because al-Asfahani refers to her as a *tharifa* (a witty woman).

Tharaf, meaning wit, humour etc., was a word used in some communities among homosexual women living in an urban environment at the time in order to describe grinding. al-Tifashi adds to this that "if one of them [the grinders] stated that so-and-so was *tharifa*, then it became known among them that she was a grinder". Similarly to how western lesbians use the word "gay," urban Arab homosexual women had the word "tharifa" which coincidently has a similar meaning to the word "gay" in that it refers to a merry or witty person. I'm going to show you now a chapter in Tifashi's book. There is a chapter that is related to grinders and it appears to be a kind of documentation or report on homosexuality amongst Arab women. And Tifashi does so in an affirmative way. In addition to his statement that female homosexual appetites may be natural, he also omits any mention of punishments or any oppressive ahadith or any moral(istic) objection to the subject. Tifashi gives us a text that is copied from a homosexual woman who also spoke about herself and Warda says:

We accompany the grinders, any one of us can be joined with one who is white, soft, flirtatious, succulent, tender-skinned as though she is a bamboo stalk, with a mouth like daisies, and ringlets like dark beads and a cheek like anemone or the apples of Lebanon and a breast like pomegranates and a stomach with four folds and a vagina that conceals fire with two lips that are coarser than the Israelite's cow and a hunch like the hump of Thamood's camel and a behind as though it is the fat-tail of Ishmael's sheep, in the colour of Ivory, and the softness of a silken garment, shaved and perfumed, anointed with musk and saffron as though it is King Anushurwan in the midst of the palace, where temples are decorated with small ringlets and the throats are ornamented with pearls and hyacinth and Yemeni slips and the Egyptian headscarfs.

So we isolate ourselves with them with impassioned reproaches and a benevolent tone, and charming eyelids that strip the heart of its blackness. So that if our chests are superimposed upon each other and the throats embrace the throats and the lips are fitted with the lips and each of them quivers against the other, then the breathing heightens and the senses are preoccupied and the fever is raised from the head, and then there would be no measure of this left, as you look for the erotic moves and the illusory consciences and the instinctual drives and the amorous civility, between sucking and pinching, and going to and fro and inhalation and sighing and moaning and murmuring and groaning, that should the people of Malta hear, they would call out: it's the bugle![5] With raising and placing and winking and suggesting, and embracing and smelling and consistency and kisses and pleasure taken in the work, and the turning of sides without worry...

All this with a royal literature and fragrant moaning, so that if unloading came and the decorations decreased, you smell like the breeze of flowers in March and the fragrances of wine in a bottle of alcohol and you look to the shaking of the ben-oil tree branch in the rain. For if the philosophers looked at what we are in, it would confuse them, while the masters of romance and delights would have been caused to fly.

Warda does not need me to comment on her words. She speaks clearly and with brilliant eroticism. She's also educated. This is evident in the fact that she refers to Quranic stories from Thamood's camel to the fat tail to Ishmail's lamb, or the cow of the Israelites. She speaks with worldly knowledge also, referring to Anu Sharwan (the Persian king) and Yemeni scarves, Egyptian headdress, as well as the people of Malta. This is not simply a cheap erotic poem. It is also an example of Arabic poetry infused with layers of intertextual meaning and literary skill, even though this poem is astonishing in its candidness and its vivid sexual representations penned probably by an Arabic grinder from 13th-century Morocco or Egypt or Syria.

And finally in this section I'd like to introduce you to a conservative Egyptian judge who dwelled in the early decades of the 13th century, and one day he found himself in a cemetery in Upper Egypt. As he was crossing the cemetery on his mule, he heard some groaning and moaning and heavy breathing coming from one of the mausoleums. What sparks my admiration in this story is the victory of the anonymous heroines, and the humiliation of the judge. I'm also interested in the description of the talk going on between the Turkish concubine and the woman having sex with her. In this story, we also observe an intriguing event: even though the women of that time were forbidden from travelling by themselves, they were still able to meet other women in their local mausoleums, in which they were not forbidden spending the night. I extrapolate then that these older Arabic homosexual women did not differ from us a great deal, in the sense that hiding, or rather invisibility was something that was forced on the (Arabic) woman in general, and what if that (Arabic) woman were to be homosexual as well? Nevertheless, these old relatives of ours did not always hide, and were not always persecuted, or afraid, or poor, or wretched, or lovely concubines. I'd like to conclude this segment with an excerpt from Tifashi:

> I witnessed one woman of them in Morocco. She had a great deal of money and a wide estate, so she spent a great deal of jewellery-money on her lover. So when she ran out of this and people began to reproach and blame her exceedingly, she warranted her lover the entire estate, which came to about five thousand dinars.

Notice here that the reproach is not due to the sex of this wealthy woman's lover, but is related to her ridiculous and rash spendings on her lover. Note also that this woman was viewed, she was visible, extroverted, and she had material independence and wealth. You may know better now why I said earlier that Aswat produces exciting literature that revives an old literary tradition.

When I read the book *Haqi An A'eesh*, I was pleased with what I found—poetic skill and humanism and a kind of consistency between the older writings and the experiences they espoused and the works of contemporary writers. On the basis of this consistency, we can pursue a liberationist strategy that is more consolidated and a political view that increases our confidence in ourselves and our self respect.

Thank you very much for your attendance, your attention, and your time. But before I release you from your chairs, I'd like to present to you a short film by the Lebanese-Australian filmmaker Fadia Abboud. Abboud won two prizes in the Annual Sydney Gay and Lesbian Mardi Gras Film Festival of 2006 for her short film, *In The Ladies Lounge*.

Fadia Abboud was born in Parramatta, a large Australian urban centre in Western Sydney and received a Bachelor of Arts in Media and Communications, becoming a filmmaker after giving up her "office" job. On her film, *In the Ladies Lounge*, she remarked that "I needed to tell this story to honour not only the women in the photograph, but the house we lived in during the last 7 years. It holds a lot of memories of queer arab comings and goings in Sydney."[6]

Abboud's film is centred around a photograph taken by a little-known Lebanese photographer, Marie el Khazen in the 1940s, which features two women dressed in English suits looking comfortably and unapologetically at the camera. Abboud soon found out more about the photographer from filmmaker Akram Zaatari who noted that "el Khazen was from an aristocratic family, she never married and died at 80 years of age, taking many photos but never thinking them worthy enough to publish. After her death, a relative pulled them out of the back of a barnyard. There are many other women in her photographs, mostly women at work, nurses around a female patient, a woman fishing, women just hanging, there is even a photograph taken in that same lounge room [as the photograph featured in *In The Ladies Lounge*], but the woman who was previously in a suit is [now] holding a baby."[7] Abboud's achievement in this short film is not only her exposure of the photographic work of this little-known, potentially lesbian, Lebanese photographer from the 1940s, but the film also simultaneously reveals a glimpse of the cultural history of contemporary Arab-Australian lesbian identity. Abboud manages to connect the two disparate times and cultures with the common experience of having a dual identity: an identity to be explored and enjoyed in private domestic spaces and another identity which accompanies spaces inhabited by heteronormativity and compulsory heterosexuality. Among some of the things present in this film that are related to my lecture is the dialogue between partial coming out, living in the domestic closet and unapologetic visibility. I particularly take note of Abboud's way of representing homosexual orientations which are also prominent Arabic identities as well.

READING THE FAMILIARITY OF THE PAST:
An Introduction to Medieval Arabic Literature on Female Homosexuality

My purpose in this brief note is to introduce the primary material upon which my research into female homosexuality in the medieval Arabian empire was based.[8] This evidence is also informative to contemporary theories of sexuality that are being propounded in the humanities. Not only does the evidence I submit inform us a great deal about the sexual lives of Arabic women of that period, but it is also relevant to present theoretical debates regarding sexual identities, which are seen, in the queer theoretical framework, as transient, as the result of "discursive structures [rather] than [being] properties of individuals."[9] What I discovered through my research and eventually became very interested in was not so much the alterity (from the modern west) of this previously unknown Arabian past, but how very often it demanded to be understood in terms far more similar to contemporary western epistemologies of sexuality than studies of western sexuality yielded about the West's own sexual past.

The title of this article and its accompanying appendix not only promises visible lesbians, but the hidden, veiled, disguised, barely visible ones of the Middle East. And there is something uncomfortably voyeuristic about this kind of interest in the Other, about fetishising or extolling their difference; it is a politics which can be both liberating and intrusive. I recall a colleague of mine referring to my work as "the epistemology of the harem" because in her mind these were the only viable places for homosexual activity between Arabian women during their hot Arabian nights, in the musk of segregated quarters belonging to some over-privileged military leader, politician or royalty.[10] Another non-Arab person, after returning from an Arab African country, commented, "I can see what you mean about female homosexuality in the Middle East: how easy is it? The women live together in separate quarters from the men." These are the mythologies of the colonists; they continue to impose their views centuries after their first colonisation of Arab populations. The cliché is that the homosexualities of the Middle East are brought on by the segregation of the sexes, and thus there are no others, like the forever celebrated "modern lesbian subject," who is "out and proud," and just adores women regardless of the nature of women's general relations to men (as oppressed or as property, etc.). In fact, views of female homosexual activity in the Middle East tend to emphasise the social "problems" that bring it about, rather than looking at the fact of lesbian sexual desire as something more permanent than cultural contexts render it.[11] Evidence of this desire, this urge for the female form, is to be found in this exemplary poem, dating back to the 9th century and possibly earlier; it reads:

> But my vagina succeeds and glimmers between a cheek and a freckle
> Like a dot of musk swinging above the crescent
> Revealing a pure mouth, smiling like pearls
> In which there is a savoury saliva
> Instantly sweet to the taste
> And a fine neck as slender as the gazelle's
>
> From what I have seen of her beauty—
> And O how much have I seen!—
> I say glory to whomever moulded beauty from clay
> To create a perfect creature made of beauty
> I came to sip from her and her extreme thirst is at a well
>
> If that is prohibited (*Haram*) then this is not lawful (*Halal*)

Note the religious symbolism of the "dot of musk swinging above the crescent," that religious image that adorns the present Pakistani flag, which is synonymous with the Islamic faith. The poet also rejects what society denies her by naming that prohibition in itself as something that is not lawful. The poet's equivocation of sexual desire with the need to quench one's thirst demonstrates a sophisticated form of reasoning, for no one would disagree that denying a thirsty person water for their thirst (particularly in the Arabian deserts) is immoral, so literal thirst becomes no different from the thirst for erotic fulfilment.

Another intriguing poem reads:

> How much have we grinded sister, ninety pilgrimages
> More delightful and invisible than the entries of the penis head,[12] and than
> A pregnancy that pleases the enemy and worse than that, the reproaches
> Of the censurers
> And we are not limited in grinding,
> Like in fornication, even though it is more
> Delicious to the inclined.[13]

What intrigues me in this poem is the "ninety" years of being a grinder,[14] the suggestion that this is a life-long process and the notion that "we are not limited in grinding, like in fornication." If the poetess was a resident of 9th-century Baghdad, we could interpret that the reference to "limitation" would mean that grinding was permitted by the Islamic jurisprudence of that period and location, while fornication was heavily punished.[15] There are several examples that suggest that some women engaged in (at least predominantly) exclusive homosexual relations, but this is most evident in a little repartee between two women, cited in Ahmad Al-Yemeni's (d. 850) chapter on grinding. One woman is evidently heterosexually inclined but abstains for fear of pregnancy (a *mutaqeeya*), and another homosexually inclined woman is imploring the *mutaqeeya* to try out grinding. The *mutaqeeya* declines this pressing invitation by reproaching the grinder for censuring (hetero-)sexual pleasures with which she is not familiar while, in the meantime, praising her own sexual preference:

> Tell her, she who recommends grinding
> How desolate is the slit against slit
> There was comfort for her in the penis
> But she has deviated from truth

> I frankly speak of your excuse and I am not indignant with you because you tried to shame what you do not know and you have proscribed what you have not tried.

This material creates quite a problem for presently widely accepted constructionist theories of sexuality that are used for studies of this kind. The emergence, or shall we say the presence of, sexual identities of a nature often understood to be Western in origin in the Middle East, confuses the understanding that exclusive and reciprocal homosexuality was a recent development.

In *Female Homosexuality in the Middle East*, I was interested in developing an essentialist project that would enable a new approach to sexuality studies within the humanities, but one which would work alongside queer theory even though it interrogates some of the conclusions of the queer theoretical framework. As Alison Eves has noted:

> More generally, queer work has re-conceptualized sexual identities as shifting and unstable, as positions offered by discursive structures rather than properties of individuals. The logical link and correspondence between biological sex, gender and desire has been challenged by theorists such as Butler (1990) so that all gender is seen as necessarily performative, suggesting alternative ways of examining the particular ways in which lesbians 'do' gender and relate to masculinity and femininity.[16]

The central tenet of queer theory has been the emphasis on difference and on variation, and at times queer theory has culminated, as we see in the above, in a theory which undermines all categories of specification as "shifting and unstable, as positions offered by discursive structures rather than properties of individuals." The effects of post-structural, deconstructive and postmodern theories on this version of sexuality-as-a- concept, has also increased a kind of institutionalisation of studies of difference, where "modern" "Western" homosexualities become incommensurable with other homosexualities—where, for example, the Ancient Greeks are understood as lovers of boys in a non-reciprocal fashion, where homosexual relations of the period are understood to be based *not* so much on desire (as we moderns understand it) but on notions that the younger man needs social advancement and the older man seeks the intellectual intimacy that women so evidently were perceived to lack.[17] This is fashioned to be different from our understanding of the "modern homosexual subject" who is characterised by his/her willingness to reciprocate and to engage in emotional and romantic relationships, and is also exclusive. It was thought that no such categories of individuals could have existed in the past, and particularly in the clandestine context of oppressed third world homosexual gatherings and activities.

Michel Foucault has had an enormous and tremendous effect on our conception of sexuality as a concept, which he argued was a 19th-century invention. In fact, Foucault is the originator of the theoretical approaches to the history of sexuality espoused in recent critical works. In distinction from essentialist consideration, Foucault wrote that:

> My aim was not to write a history of sexual behaviors and practices, tracing their successive forms, their evolution, and their dissemination; nor was it to analyze the scientific, religious, or philosophical ideas through which these behaviors have been represented. I wanted first to dwell on that quite recent and banal notion of "sexuality": to stand detached from it, bracketing its familiarity, in order to analyze the theoretical and practical context with which it has been associated. The term itself did not appear until the beginning of the nineteenth century, a fact that should be neither underestimated nor overinterpreted. It does point to something other than a simple recasting of vocabulary, but obviously it does not mark the sudden emergence of that to which "sexuality" refers.[18]

But these Foucauldian ideas *were* over-interpreted in the sense that emphasis was granted to the idea that the history of sexuality revealed "something other than a simple recasting of vocabulary" when it came to the formation of sexual identities and self-knowledge, while, in the meantime, the balancing remainder of that idea was neglected, that being that the recent history of sexuality discourse did *not* "mark the sudden emergence of that to which 'sexuality' refers."

It is precisely this reluctance—prevalent in contemporary criticism—to accept that contemporary vocabulary *can* be used to inform us about the past, to which I am drawing attention. It is not the Foucauldian idea that the concept of "sexuality" has a short-lived history in itself, but I remain sceptical of Foucault's conclusion that sexuality was *erroneously* "conceived of as a constant" (4), if only because "that to which 'sexuality' refers" *is* a constant which can be easily seen, though unexpectedly, in the case study of female homosexuality in medieval Arabia. Perhaps ultimately we are doomed to give a name (an arbitrary signifier as Nietzsche has suggested?[19]) to these nameless phenomena, and though the names may be arbitrary, to which permanent fixtures are they referring? What is beneath the discursive stagings of culture? Female homosexual desire is certainly one of those fixtures.

Misunderstanding Female Homosexuality in the Middle East

When hearing that I was particularly looking into Islamic civilisation and culture, some people were keen to hear about the gruesome punishments inflicted on those who were caught in the act—beheadings, stoning, hanging, honour-killings—and these things do happen, but not in a magnitude proportionate to the Western media's focus on them when addressing homosexuality in the contemporary Arab world. I am sure that something angled like Irshad Manji's bereft scholarship in *The Trouble With Islam* would have gone down well, would have satisfied expectations of the "degeneracy" of Muslim nations living in what she, in my opinion, insultingly calls the "grip of desert tribalism."[20]

But my research has not met the expectations of those who sought to be reminded of the inferiority of the Middle East when it comes to civil liberties, in a way which was unconnected from the West's imperial role in that degeneration. In fact, by understanding earlier Islamic cultures and the variety and heterogeneity of contemporary ones in relation to female homosexuality in that region, we come to a deeper appreciation and understanding of the Arab world—a world which outwardly appears repressive, closed, immutable, but which reveals dynamic inconsistencies, underworlds of resistance and subversion.

Medieval poetry on the subject of Arabian homosexuality was divided by anthologists of the period between categories of censure and categories of praise. This is particularly evident in Tifashi's work, translated in the appendix to this article. One example from the category of censure:

> God damn you, you unfaithful whore
> How do you rub your pubis with another pubis
> When every house that is covered by a ceiling
> Must have a pillar in the middle of it?

While a medieval queer response to this genre of censure was fashioned, it has only survived in Tifashi's collection, and in an instance in the *Arabian Nights* which Richard Burton translated in the 19th century:

> The penis smooth and round was made/with anus best to match it/ Had it been made for cunnus' sake, / it had been formed like a hatchet.[21]

Not only was there a rich collection of material which spoke of homosexual desire, but it appears as though medieval scholars writing on the subject were engaging with concerns over whether homosexuality was innate or socially produced (see Tifashi and Samaw'uli), whether it was an illness or natural, whether it was reversible or permanent.

In the 13th century, Ahmad Ibn Yusuf al-Tifashi (a Muslim scholar) demonstrates that there was no homological view, no single condemnatory stance being advanced at every juncture of his anecdotes. On the contrary, if Tifashi's sensibility is anything to go by, there was an admiration reserved for some of the women known as grinders, who were often educated scholars of Islam, as well as musicians and entertainers, and who were both slave girls and free women.

Further to their discourse regarding whether homosexuality is innate or constructed, I discovered that medieval Muslim scholars engaging in this subject were seeking to devise categories of female homosexuality. The group of lesbians akin to modern day "butches" were then known as *mutathakirat*, although some of them are very likely to have been transsexual individuals, or, from the descriptions of their hypertrophied "clitorises" (that remind us of the studies of 17th- and 18th-century western tribades) they may have been intersexed.[22] In fact, the whole person of the tribade in the description of "her" physique is more convincing if read as a "male pseudo-hermaphrodite"—an intersexed individual whose anatomy fits the description much better than the mythological "lesbian" clitoris we have been reading through the figure of the tribade, and now may be perceiving through the figure of the *mutathakirat*. Note for example the following descriptions of these "butches" possessing hypertrophied clitorises:

> They have said: When she is erect something comes out from under her stomach that looks like a cock's comb. However this description is not accurate: it is a thin bone which is found above the penis-entrance [i.e. vagina],

> which resembles the nose bone. She climbs up on the vagina of her passive subject and she rubs her with it. When she does this they both feel a pleasure greater than marriage—the pleasure is greater for the active one. When she rubs against the vagina of the woman to whom this is done, then it emerges quite significantly like baby-teeth, except that it is long not wide, and they both find a pleasure greater than what is to be found in marriage.

In fact, al-Yemeni is arguing here that there is no such thing as the "mythological" cock's comb (or the hypertrophied clitoris of the tribade) and instead he asserts that all men can discover these particular parts of the anatomy (i.e. the clitoris): "And if the man intended that particular place [above the vaginal entrance] in the woman with his penis then it would appear for him and he would see from her pleasure and her disintegration what I have here mentioned."

Among these *mutathakirat*, there were *women* who did not sport enlarged clitorises but who continued to take on what was labelled as "the mannerisms of the man" and who were also lovers of other women:

> There are some of them who exceed others in intelligence and deception and in their nature there is much that resembles men. So much so that one of them might resemble men in her movements and her speech and her voice. Such a woman is a lover [as opposed to being beloved] because she is the active partner and so she needs someone she can be on top of and not be ashamed to seduce every time her appetite is roused. It does not suit

> her to have intercourse at the time where her appetite is dormant. So this, together with the difficulty in cumming under the pleasures and command of the man, leads her to grinding. The greatest number of those who possess these traits are among the witty women, and the writers and the Quranic readers and the scholars. Some of them are drawn to grinding due to the intensity of restriction imposed on them, where they are unable to be alone safely and privately except with other women. (Samaw'uli)

Celebrated as the signpost of lesbian visibility, as an alternative to mainstream masculinity, subversive and transgressive, butch lesbians have also been the subject of much ridicule, of having penis envy, of either wanting to be men or of hating and competing with men, or of re-inscribing or imitating a heteronormative paradigm. I could not help when preparing this paper but to see the trope of the butch lesbian as facilitating the search for patterns. Although many female masculinities are not homosexually oriented and many of those masculinities which appear to be female can be in fact male on either a psychic or physical level, nevertheless, we should be comfortable in stating that there are many lesbian butches out there, and a culturally specific approach to the trope of the butch lesbian cannot tell us what the transhistorical and transcultural similarities really mean.

My intention in making this material available to the international academic community is to reinvigorate a debate which has reached a kind of impasse: if everything is constructed by humans and their respective societies, then what is the underlying pre-linguistic something about which we build these constructions?

I hope that the material presented in the appendix will help us to begin to answer these intriguing essentialist questions which have been much neglected due to their seeming impossibility.[23]

READING THE FAMILIARITY OF THE PAST (ARABIC)

الحرية الجنسية في الأيام الغابرة: مقدّمة تعرض كتابات القرون العربية الوسطى في المثلية الجنسية عند النساء

هدفي من هذا النص هو عرض المواد الأولية التي بنيت عليها بحثي في المثلية الجنسية عند النساء خلال الامبراطورية العربية في القرون الوسطى[24]. فهو يعتبر دليلاً تثقيفياً يدعم النظريات المعاصرة للجنس، التي يتمّ تداولها اليوم بين الاكاديميين في العلوم الانسانية. المعلومات التي أعرضها في هذا النص لا تعطينا فكرة فقط عن الحياة الجنسية للنساء العرب في تلك الفترة وإنّما تصلح لتثير اليوم نقاشات نظرية حول الهويات الجنسية المختلفة في إطار نظرية تحرير الجنس (queer theory) التي تعتبر ان الهوية الجنسية هي نتيجة هيكليات استطرادية (discourse) و ليست ملك للأشخاص،"[25] في الواقع، ما اكتشفته من خلال هذا البحث وما جذبني فعلاً لمعرفة المزيد ليس اختلاف هذا الماضي العربي عن الغرب العصري وإنّما هو مدى حاجة هذا الماضي إلى أشخاص يحسنون مقاربته بمفهوم الجنس الغربي المعاصر أكثر من أن يندرج في دراسات الجنس الغربي التي تناولت تاريخ الحياة الجنسية في الغرب نفسه.

لا يشير عنوان هذا النص ومرفقاته إلى السحاقيات لاسباب اثارة رخيصة ، وإنّما أردت من خلاله توجيه الأنظار نحو السحاقيات المخبات والمحجبات والمتنكرات وغير المرئيات في الشرق الأوسط. ويعتري هذا الاهتمام بالآخر نوع من اللذة الذي تكون اقتحامية وتحرّرية في آن معاً. وأذكر أنّ زميلة لي قد أطلقت على عملي هذا تسمية "نظرية معرفة الحريم" لأنها في مفهومها لهذا الموضوع تعتبر الحريم هو المكان الوحيد الذي يسمح بالنشاطات الجنسية المثلية بين النساء خلال الليالي الحمراء الحارّة وذلك في جوّ من المسك يعطّر الأقسام المنفصلة لمنزل أحد الزعماء العسكريين الرفيعي المستوى أو أحد السياسيين أو أفراد من العائلة المالكة (لا يحسد عليه أبداً!)[26]. كما أعربت إمرأة عربية غير عودتها إثر عودتها من بلد عربي إفريقي عن رأيها في هذا الموضوع قائلةً: "الآن عرفت ماذا تعنين بالمثلية الجنسية عند النساء في الشرق الأوسط، وكم هو أمر سهل؟ فالنساء يعشن معاً في أقسام منفصلة عن الرجال". ويأتي هذا التقليد من ميتولوجيات المستعمرين في تلك العصور حيث استمرّ هؤلاء بفرض مفاهيمهم لقرون عدّة بعد استعمار الشعوب العربية للمرة الأولى. الفكرة المتداولة هي أنّ سبب المثلية الجنسية في الشرق الأوسط هي عزل الجنسين وفصلهما عن بعضهما البعض، في اعتقاد العديد من المفكرين اصبحت المثلية المعاصرة مختلفة عن تصوير المثلية عند العرب. في الواقع، عند مقاربة موضوع النشاط الجنسي المثلي عند النساء في الشرق الأوسط، يميل البعض إلى التركيز على المشاكل الاجتماعية المسبّبة و لكن هذه الرغبة الجنسية دائمة أكثر من السياق الثقافي الذي تندرج فيه.[27] مثال على هذه الرغبة، على هذا الجموح نحو المرأة، في هذا الشعر الذي يعود إلى القرن التاسع وعلى الأرجح قبله، ويقول:

لكن كسى يجود يزهو بخد وخال
كمثل نقطة مسك تلوح فوق هلال
تريك ثغراً نقياً ومبسماً كاللآلئ
فيه رضاب شهي عذب المذاقة حالي

وحسن جيد بهي كمثل جيد الغزال
أقول لمن بدا لي من حسنها يا ما بدا لي
سبحان من صاغ الجمال من صلصال
فصار خلقاً سوياً مكوناً من جمال
أتيت أرشف فيها وصادها عند دال
إن كان هذا حرام فذاك غير حلال

تجدر الإشارة إلى أنّ عبارة "نقطة مسك تلوح فوق هلال" هي صورة دينية تزيّن العلم الباكستاني الحالي وهي مرادف للإيمان الإسلامي. كما ترفض الكاتبة ما ينهيها المجتمع عن فعله بالقول إن كان هذا حرام فذاك غير حلال. المعادلة التي تعرضها الكاتبة بين الرغبة الجنسية والحاجة لإرواء ظمأ الآخر يظهر تكلّفاً كبيراً في طريقة التحليل إذ لا يمكن نكران أنّ رفض إرواء ظمأ عطشان (بخاصة في الصحارى العربية) هو عمل لا أخلاقي، لذا اعتماد الحرفية في ذكر الظمأ تجعل فعل إرواء العطش الجنسي الشهواني لا يقلّ أهمية عن إرواء عطش أحدهم إلى الماء.

هذا شعر آخر يندرج في السياق نفسه:

وكم قد سحقنا، أخت، تسعين حجة   أسرّ اخفي من دون دخول الفياشل[28]
ومن حبل يرضي العدو ظهوره   وأعظم من هذا ملام العوازل
وليس علينا الحد في السحق كالزنا   وإن كان أشهى منه عند القوابل[29]

ما يثير انتباهي في هذا الشعر هو "تسعين حجة" أي تسعون عاماً من السحق[30]، مما يشير إلى أنّ السحق مشوار حياة؛ وفكرة أنّه "ليس علينا الحد في السحق كالزنا" تعطي الانطباع أنّه في بغداد حيث في القرن التاسع كانت الشريعة الإسلامية في ذاك الزمان والمكان تسمح بالسحاق في حين كان العقاب شديداً في حال الزنا.[31] أمثلة عديدة متوفرة تبيّن انخراط النساء في علاقات جنسية مثلية وحصرية (أقلّه بأغلبيتهنّ) وهو جليّ في براعة الإجابة في الحوار بين المرأتين، كما ذكر أحمد اليمني (850) في الفصل المتعلّق بالسحق: بديهي أن تكون المرأة تميل للتغاير جنسياً لكنها تمتنع عن ذلك خوفاً من أن تصبح حاملاً (متقية) وأخرى تميل إلى المثلية تناشد المتقية أن تجرّب السحق. فترفض المتقية هذه الدعوة اللجوجة عبر تأنيب السحاقية لضبط الملذات الجنسية المائلة إلى التغاير وهو أمر ليست بعرفه ، فلعلوم الملائية في الوقت عينه من خلال التسمية بالتعبير عن تفضيلها الجنسي:

قولوا المستحسنة السحق
ما أوحش الشق على الشق
قد كان في الأير لها راحة
لكنها زاغت عن الحق
ثم إني لعذرك باسطة، وغير ساخطة، لأنّك عبثَ ما لا تعرفين، ونهيت عما لا تخبرين

تطرح هذه المواد إشكالية فعلية بالنسبة إلى النظريات الحالية البنّاءة (constructionist) والمقبولة بشكل عام من الجميع، التي تتناول موضوع الجنس ويعتمد عليها في دراسات من هذا النوع. ظهور أو يمكن القول أيضاً وجود هويات جنسية "غربية الشكل" في الشرق الأوسط القديم يشوّش المفهوم القائل بأنّ المثلية الجنسية الحصرية والمتبادلة هو تطوّر جديد.

همّني في كتاب "المثلية الجنسية عند النساء في الشرق الأوسط" أن أضع برنامجاً جديد لنظرية الأساسية (essentialism) لأمكّن الباحثين من وضع مقاربة جديدة للدراسات حول الجنس في إطار العلوم الثقافية متماشياً مع نظرية تحرير الجنس حتّى ولو أنّه يتناقض مع بعض الاستنتاجات النهائية لهذه النظرية. فكما أوردت أليسون إيف:

عرضت نظرية تحرير الجنس أن الهويات الجنسية متقلبة و غير مستقرة، تنتج من هيكالات استعرادية وليست ملك للاشخاص. و تحدى الباحثون، كي جودث بتلر، العلاقة المنطقية بين جنس الجسد البيولوجي و جنس العقل والرغبة الجنسية، قائلون أن الجنسة هي دائماً شيء استعراضي. و يؤدي ذلك إلى استكشاف المثليات للمزيد من الطرق للتعبير عن الذكورة و الانوثة

قد كان المعتقد الرئيسي لنظرية تحرير الجنس هو التركيز على الاختلاف والتغاير وفي بعض الأحيان كانت النظرية تبلغ حدّها الأقصى كما هو مذكور أعلاه حيث تقلّل من قدرة الفئات كلّها بوصفها " متقلّبة وغير مستقرّة، وانها نتيجة هيكليات استعرادية وليست ملك للأشخاص". مفاعيل النظريات ما بعد-الهيكلية (-post structuralism) والهدامة (deconstruction) وما بعد العصرية (postmodernism) ادت الى تاسيس فكرة ان الجنس هو مجرد مفاهيم فقط وقد ضاعفت التركيز على دراسة الاختلاف حيث أصبحت المثلية الجنسية الغربية المعاصرة غير قابلة للمقاربة مع الأنواع الأخرى من المثلية الجنسية. فعلى سبيل المثال، قيل عن اليونانيين القدامى أنهم عشاق الصبيان ضمن تقليد يفرض عدم مبادلة الشعور من جهة ومن جهة أخرى لا ترتكز علاقاتهم المثلية هذه بشكل أساسي على الرغبة (كما يعتبرها المعاصرون اليوم) بل هي عبارة عن معادلة تشير إلى حاجة الصبيان إلى التقدّم الاجتماعي والرجال الأكبر سناً بحاجة إلى صداقات حميمة وفكرية وهو أمر كان يعتقد أن النساء كنّ يفتقدنه في تلك الفترة[32]. إن هذا التفسير مختلف عن مفاهيمنا لموضوع "المثلية الجنسية المعاصرة" التي تتميّز بإصرار الشخص (ذكراً أم أنثى) على التبادل في العلاقة والدخول في علاقات عاطفية ورومنسية حصرية. كان يعتقد أن هذا النوع من العلاقات لم يكن موجوداً في الماضي بخاصة في الإطار السري للتجمعات والنشاطات المقموعة في العالم الثالث.

وقد كان لمايكل فوكو تأثيركبير وهائل على مفهوم الجنس اليوم، الذي كان يعتبره اختراع القرن التاسع عشر. ففوكو هو واضع المقاربات النظرية لتاريخ الجنس اللتي تستعمل حتى اليوم. وفي توجه يتناقد مع نظرية الاساسية (essentialism)و يكتب :

ما كان هدفي هو كتابة تاريخ السلوكيات والممارسات الجنسية وتتبّع أشكالها المتلاحقة، وتطوّرها وانتشارها. والهدف لم يكن يوماً تحليل الأفكار الفلسفية والدينية والعلمية التي من خلالها تمّ تقديم هذه السلوكيات. أردت أولاً الإمعان في النظرية الأخيرة التافهة للجنسية (sexuality): أن أكون منفصلاً عنها، أحدّد حميميتها من أجل التمكّن من تحليل السياق العملي والنظري المرتبط بها. لم تظهر التسمية بحدّ ذاتها قبل القرن التاسع عشر، وهو أمر لا يجدر التقليل من أهميتها كما أنّه لا يجب إعطاؤه حجماً أكبر من حجمه. فهو يدلّ على شيء أبعد من إعادة صياغة المفردات بكل بساطة، بل هو جليّ أنّه لا يميّز البروز المفاجئ للمفهوم الذي تعبّر عنه كلمة "الجنسية".(sexuality) 3

لكنّه تمّ الافراط في تفسير أفكار فوكو هذه بمعنى أنّ تمّ التركيز على الفكرة أن تاريخ الجنس في ما يتعلّق بتكوين الهويات الجنسية والمعرفة الذاتية يبيّن ما هو أبعد من إعادة صياغة بسيطة للمفردات. في حين أنّه في الوقت عينه، تمّ إهمال عامل توازن هذه الفكرة، الذي يتجسّد في أن التاريخ الحديث للمسيرة الجنسية لم يميّز البروز المفاجئ لما تجسده كلمة "الجنسية" (sexuality).

وهنا انتقد المقاومة التي ترفض إمكانية تقبّل المفردات المعاصرة التي يمكن اللجوء إليها لمعرفة المزيد عن ماض يتشابه مع هويات جنسية معاصرة. لست اعارض فكرة فوكو أنّ مفهوم الجنسية له تاريخ قصير بحدّ ذاته، ولكنني أشكّك دوماً في استنتاج فوكو القائل بأنّ الجنسية (4) ليست ثابتة معيّنة مع أنّ الجنس يشير إلى ثابتة يسهل علينا رؤيتها في دراسة قضية المثلية الجنسية عند النساء في البلاد العربية في القرون الوسطى. وربّما أنّنا محكومون بإيجاد تسمية لهذه الظواهر التي ليس لها إسم (مدلول اعتباطي كما أشار نيتشي[33]) وهل يمكن أن تكون التسميات اعتباطية أيضاً في دلالتها إلى المظاهر الثابتة التي تعبّر عنها؟ ماذا بعد المراحل استعرادية للثقافة؟ فالمثلية الجنسية عند النساء هي حتماً واحدة من هذه المظاهر الموجودة عبر التاريخ .

سوء فهم المثلية الجنسية عند النساء في الشرق الأوسط

كلَّما عرف أحدهم أنَّني أتناول موضوع الثقافة والحضارة الإسلامية، كان يبدو متحمّساً لمعرفة العقاب الرهيب التي كان يُفرض على أولئك الذين يمسكون بالجرم المشهود – أهو عقاب بقطع الرأس أو الرجم، أو الشنق، أو جرائم الشرف. في الواقع، تحصل هذه الأمور ولكن بقدر نسبي مقارنة مع تركيز الإعلام الغربي على هذه المسائل في تناوله المثلية الجنسية في العالم العربي. وأنا متأكّدة أنَّ شيئاً شبيهاً لمنحة إرشاد منحني في "المشكلة مع الإسلام" قد كان لينجح فعلاً، ولكن هل كان لبروي تطلّعات بانحلال: الأمم الإسلامية التي تعيش في ما أسماه بتهكّم "قبضة العصبية القبلية الصحراوية" 34

غير أنَّ بحثي لم يكن على مستوى توقّعات الذين ظنّوا أنَّه سيذكّرهم بعقدة نقص الشرق الأوسط في ما يتعلَّق بالحريات المدنية بطريقة كان فيها غير مرتبط بالدور الغربي الملكي خلال ذلك الانحلال. في الحقيقة، عبر فهم الثقافات العربية الأقدم وتشكيلة المعاصر منها المتعلّقة بالمثلية الجنسية عند النساء وتنوّعها في العالم العربي، نصل إلى فهم أعمق وتقدير أكبر للعالم العربي. هذا العالم الذي يبدو من الخارج قامعاً مغلقاً وجامداً، يخفي في طيّاته تناقضات ديناميكية – عالم آخر من المقاومة وتدمير للنظام.

قسّم جامعو المقتطفات الأدبية الشعر في القرون الوسطى، الذي يتناول المثلية الجنسية العربية إلى فئات من النقد مقابل فئات من المديح، وهذا النوع من الشعر يظهر جلياً في عمل تيفاشي المترجم في ملحق هذا النص. مثال على فئات النقد:

كم تدلكين عانة بعانة   ويلك يا قحبة يا خيانة
لا بد في وسطه اسطوانة   وكلّ بيت حواه سقف

على الرغم من انتشار تجاوب متحرر في القرون الوسطى مع هذا النوع الأدبي النقدي، لم يستمرّ هذا الأخير إلا في مجموعة تيفاشي ولفترة معينة في كتاب ألف ليلة وليلة التي ترجمها ريتشارد بورتون بشكل غني جداً في القرن التاسع عشر:

كان القضيب ناعماً مدوّراً/ و الدبر يناسب شكله / وإن كان للفرج لكان كالبليطة 35

إلى جانب وجود مجموعة غنية من المؤلفات التي تناولت موضوع رغبات المثلية الجنسية، بدا علماء القرون الوسطى مهتمين بموضوع ما إذا كانت المثلية الجنسية فطرية أو نتيجة حالة اجتماعية معيّنة (العودة إلى تيفاشي وسومالي)، وما إذا كانت المثلية الجنسية مرضاً أو حالة طبيعية، وما إذا كانت حالة يمكن عكسها أو هي حالة دائمة.

في القرن الثالث عشر، بيّن أحمد بن يوسف التيفاشي (عالم مسلم) أنَّ عدم وجود أيّ تماثل أو أيّ موقف واحد يدينه في أيّ مفصل من مفاصل حكاياته. بل هو على العكس، إذا كانت له مشاعر معيّنة، فهي إعجاب لبعض النساء السحاقيات اللواتي غالباً ما كنَّ عالمات مثقفات في الإسلام أو موسيقيات ومغنيات وفي الوقت عينه مستعبدات ونساء حرّات.

وفي معالجتهم لموضوع المثلية الجنسية ما إذا كانت فطرية أم نتيجة حالة معيّنة، اكتشفت أنَّ العلماء المسلمين في القرون الوسطى كانوا يسعون إلى تقسيم المثلية الجنسية النسائية إلى فئات. فمجموعة النساء المماثلة "للمسترجلات" في أيامنا الحالية، كانت تسمّى المتذكرات مع أنّها في بعض الأحيان المتذكرات هم مغايرات

الجنس ، أو من خلال وصف البظر المتضخّم (ما يذكرنا بالدراسات التي تناولت موضوع الـtribades في قرون السابعة و الثامنة عشر). [36] في الواقع، يكون الوصف الكامل لمظهر هذه "المرأة" مقنعاً أكثر إذا سميت حالته/ا بـ male pseudo-hermaphrodite – أي شخص مزدوج الجنس يتلاءم تكوينه مع الوصف الذي أشرنا إليه أكثر منه مع بظر السحاقيات الأسطوري الذي قرأنا عنه في صورة الـtribade ونلاحظه هنا من خلال وصف بعض المتذكرات. تجدر الإشارة أيضاً إلى الوصف التالي للمتذكرات الذي يظهر فيهن البظر المتضخّم:

قالوا: وإنعاظها أن يخرج لها تحت البطن شيء كعرف الديك، وليس كذلك، وإنما هو العظم الرقيق الذي فوق مدخل الأير، تشبه الأنف الداخل في ليّنة يسمونه العنصب، فتصعد على فرج المفعول بها وتحك به، فإذا حكت به وجدت بينهما لذة أشد من لذة النكاح وللفاعلة أكثر، فإذا حكت به فرج المفعول بها برز بروزاً شديداً   كدردر الطفل إلا أنّه مستطيل غير معترض، ويجدان له لذة أعظم من لذة النكاح. وإذا تعمد الرجل ذلك الموضع من المرأة بأيره برز له ذلك، ورأى من التذاذها وانحلالها ما يدل على ما ذكرت، وقد تدمى حجر الأمرد.

في الواقع، يعرض اليمني حججاً ليثبت أنّ لا وجود لما هو معروف بعرف الديك الأسطوري (أو البظر المتضخّم للـtribade) وبدل ذلك أكّد أنّه يمكن لكل الرجال اكتشاف هذه المناطق المحددة من جسم المرأة (أي البظر): "وإذا قصد الرجل تحسّس هذا المكان من جسد المرأة بقضيبه [فوق مدخل الرحم] ستتوضّح له الفكرة التي أشير إليها وتتجلّى له بوضوح من خلال لذّتها بذلك ومن خلال انحلالها".

ومن بين المتذكرات *نساء*، اللواتي ليس لديهن بظراً متضخماً ولكنّهن يصفن كمتذكرات.

ومنهن من تفوق غيرها في الذكاء والخبّ وفي طبعها كثير من أخلاق الرجال حتّى أنّها ربما أشبهتهم في حركاتها وكلامها وصوتها وتكون محبّة لأن تكون هي الفاعلة فهي تريد من يمكّنها بحيث تعلوه ولا تحتشم عن المراودة كلّما تحركت غلمتها ولا يسوسها الجماع وقت سكون شهرتها فيخرجها ذلك مع استصعاب النزول تحت مراضي الرجل وحكمه إليّ السحق وأكثر أصحاب هذه الصفات من المتظرّفات والكاتبات والمقرّنات والعالمات ومنهنّ من يلجيها إلى السحق شدّة الحجر عليها فلا يتهيا لها الخلوة مع ستر وأمن بغير النساء.

عرفت المثليات المتذكرات كدليل في مقاربة موضوع المثلية وكبديل للاتجاه الذكوري السائد. كما أصبحت هذه المثليات سبباً لنوع من السخرية لجهة الشعور بالرغبة بالقضيب وبالرغبة بأن تكون رجلاً وبأن تكره وتنافس الرجال أو بأن تقوم بتقليد أو بإعادة تشكيل نموذج المغايرة. لم أستطع خلال تحضيري لهذا البحث إلاّ أن أنظر إلى مجاز المثليات المتذكرات في تسهيل التفتيش عن نموذج الأساسية. مع أنّ العديد من النساء المتذكرات لسن مثليات جنسياً والكثير منهن يظهرن بمظهر المرأة وهنّ في الواقع ذكوراً على المستوى النفسي أو الجسدي، علينا أن نشعر بحرية الاعتراف بوجود هؤلاء النساء المتذكرات المثليات، وأنّه لا يمكن لمقاربة ثقافية محددة لمجاز المثليات المتذكرات أن تحدد فعلاً ماذا تعني هذه التشبيهات عبر ثقافات و تواريخ متعددة.

هدفي من خلال توفير هذه المادة للمجتمع الأكاديمي العالمي هو إعادة فتح نقاش واجه في الآونة الأخيرة طريقاً مسدوداً ؛ فإذا كان كلّ شيء في هذه الدنيا قد بناه البشر أنفسهم وبفعل مجتمعاتهم، إذن ما هو هذا الشيء المخفي ما قبل اللغة الذي نبني عليه هذه التفسيرات؟ آمل أن تساعدنا هذه المواد التي اقدمها في البدء بالإجابة على الأسئلة المثيرة للاهتمام والأساسية التي تمّ إهمالها طويلاً بسبب استحالتها الظاهرية.

LECTURE DE LA FAMILIARITÉ DU PASSÉ :

Introduction à la Littérature Arabe Médiévale sur l'Homosexualité des Femmes

Le but du présent article est de présenter les documents qui ont informé notre recherche sur la question de l'homosexualité des femmes dans l'empire arabe médiéval.[37] Nous avançons que ces documents sont également utiles aux théories contemporaines sur la sexualité dans les sciences humaines. Non seulement ils nous donnent énormément d'informations sur la sexualité des femmes arabes de cette période, ils sont également pertinents aux débats théoriques actuels sur les identités sexuelles qui, dans le cadre théorique de l'homosexualité, sont considérées comme transitoires, comme le résultat de "structures discursives [plutôt] que de caractéristiques d'individus."[38] Notre recherche montre que – et c'est cela que nous trouvons particulièrement intéressant- ce n'est pas tant l'altérité (de l'Occident moderne) de ce passé arabe précédemment inconnu, mais la nécessité de le comprendre en termes beaucoup plus similaires à ceux de l'épistémologie occidentale contemporaine de la sexualité que ne l'a fait jusqu'à présent les études sur la sexualité occidentale, en ce qui concerne le passé sexuel de l'Occident lui-même.

Le titre du présent article et son annexe promettent non seulement de parler des lesbiennes, et comment elles peuvent être visuellement appréciées par plusieurs d'entre nous, mais aussi être cachées, voilées, déguisées et à peine visibles au Moyen Orient. Et il y a quelque chose d'inconfortable et de voyeur dans ce genre d'intérêt que l'on accorde à l'autre, dans ce fétichisme ou cette célébration de la différence de l'autre, politique qui peut être à la fois libératrice et intrusive. Nous nous souvenons d'une collègue faisant référence à notre recherche comme une forme d'"épistémologie du harem", parce que, dans son esprit, les harems sont les seuls lieux d'activité homosexuelle entre femmes arabes pendant leurs chaudes Nuits d'Arabie, dans le musc de résidences séparées appartenant à quelque chef militaire, politicien ou membre de la famille royale (non enviable quelque soit la catégorie !).[39] De retour d'un pays arabe d'Afrique, une autre personne non Arabe avait déclaré, "Je comprends ce que vous dites au sujet de l'homosexualité des femmes au Moyen Orient. Comme c'est facile pour elles ! Les femmes vivent ensemble dans des résidences séparées de celles des hommes." Mais ce ne sont là que des exemples des mythologies des colons qui continuent d'imposer leurs points de vue sur les populations arabes, des siècles après la colonisation. Le cliché est que l'homosexualité au Moyen Orient est le résultat de la ségrégation des sexes, et qu'il n'y a par conséquent pas de cas semblables au célèbre « sujet lesbien moderne » qui "ne cache pas son homosexualité et est fier," et adore tout simplement les femmes sans s'appesantir sur la nature des relations générales des femmes vis-à-vis des hommes (comme opprimées ou comme propriété, etc.). En fait, les points de vue sur l'activité homosexuelle des femmes au Moyen Orient tendent à mettre l'accent sur les "problèmes" sociaux à l'origine de celle-ci, plutôt que de considérer le fait que le désir sexuel lesbien est quelque chose de plus permanent que le contexte culturel.40 La preuve de ce désir, de cette impulsion pour la forme féminine est décrite dans ce poème exemplaire, datant du neuvième siècle, et peut être même avant :

> ...mon vagin a du succès et luit faiblement entre une joue et une tache de rousseur
> Comme un point de musc oscillant au dessus du croissant
> Révélant une bouche pure, des perles souriantes
> Dans laquelle il y a une salive savoureuse instamment douce au goût.
> Et un beau cou aussi effilé que celui d'une gazelle
>
> Pour ce que j'ai vu de sa beauté –
> Et O combien j'en ai vu ! –
> Je dis gloire à quiconque a façonné l'argile
> Pour créer une parfaite créature de beauté
> Je suis venu siroter d'elle et de sa soif extrême au puits
>
> Si cela est interdit (*Haram*), alors cela est illégal (*Halal*)

On notera les symboles religieux tel que "point de musc oscillant au dessus du croissant ;" cette image religieuse que l'on retrouve sur le drapeau pakistanais actuel, et qui est synonyme de la foi islamique. La poétesse rejette également ce que la société lui nie et dit de cette interdiction qu'elle est illégale. L'équivoque du désir sexuel de la poétesse et le besoin de satisfaire à cette soif démontre une forme sophistiquée de raisonnement, et personne ne niera que refuser de l'eau à une personne assoiffée (particulièrement dans les déserts arabes) est immoral. Ainsi, la soif, au sens littéral du mot, n'est pas différente de la soif de satisfaction érotique.

Dans un autre poème bizarre, on peut lire ce qui suit :

> Comme nous avons bien baisé ma soeur, quatre vingt dix pèlerinages
> Plus merveilleux et invisibles que les allées et venues d'une tête de pénis[41] ; et puis
> Une grossesse qui plait à l'ennemi et pire encore, les reproches
> Des critiques
> Et nous ne sommes pas limitées dans nos actes,
> Comme dans le cas de la fornication, bien que celle-ci soit plus
> délicieuse pour ceux qui la préfèrent.[42]

Ce que nous trouvons bizarre dans ce poème, ce sont les "quatre vingt dix" années que l'on a passé à bien baiser,[43] la suggestion qu'il s'agit là d'un long processus qui dure toute une vie, et la notion que "nous ne sommes pas limitées dans nos actes, comme dans la fornication." Si la poétesse était une résidente de Bagdad au neuvième siècle, on pourrait dire que la référence à la 'limitation' voudrait dire que la copulation était permise par la jurisprudence islamique de cette période et de ce locus, alors que la fornication était sévèrement punie.[44] Il y a plusieurs exemples suggérant que les femmes avaient exclusivement des relations homosexuelles, ou du moins de façon prédominante, mais cela est beaucoup plus évident dans une petite réplique entre deux femmes, citée dans le chapitre d'Ahmad Al-Yemeni (d. 850) sur la copulation. Une femme a évidemment des penchants hétérosexuels, mais s'abstient de peur de tomber enceinte (une mutaqeeya) et une autre femme aux penchants homosexuels implore la mutaqeeya de s'essayer à la copulation. La mutaqeeya décline cette pressante invitation et reproche à cette dernière de censurer les plaisirs (hétéro)sexuels dont elle n'est pas familière, alors qu'en même temps elle loue sa propre préférence sexuelle :

> Dis-lui, à celle qui recommande la copulation
> Comme il est désolant d'avoir fente contre fente
> Elle trouvait du confort dans le pénis
> Mais elle était détournée de la vérité

> Je parle franchement de votre excuse et je ne suis pas indignée, parce que vous avez essayé de déshonorer ce que vous ne connaissez pas et vous avez interdit ce que vous n'avez pas essayé.

Ce document pose un sérieux problème en ce qui concerne les théories constructivistes de la sexualité généralement acceptées dans ce genre d'études. L'émergence, ou plutôt la présence d'identités sexuelles d'une nature souvent considérée comme occidentale d'origine au Moyen Orient, bouleverse l'entendement selon lequel l'homosexualité exclusive et réciproque est le résultat de développements récents.

Dans *Homosexualité des femmes au Moyen Orient* nous voulions mettre en avant un projet essentialiste qui permettrait d'adopter une nouvelle approche à la sexualité dans les sciences humaines, et qui fonctionnerait en parallèle avec la théorie de l'homosexualité, bien qu'elle remet en question certaines des conclusions de cette dernière. Comme le remarque Alison Eves :

> D'une manière générale, les travaux de recherche sur l'homosexualité ont re-conceptualisé les identités sexuelles comme changeantes et instables, comme des positions offertes par des structures discursives, plutôt que des propriétés d'individus. Le lien logique et la correspondance entre le sexe biologique, le rôle de la femme et de l'homme et le désir ont été remis en question par des théoriciens tels que Butler (1990) ; de telle sorte que le sexe est considéré comme nécessairement performatif, suggérant des alternatives dans l'examen des approches particulières avec lesquelles les lesbiennes 'traitent' le sexe et comprennent la masculinité et la féminité. 481-482

Le principe fondamental de la théorie de l'homosexualité est l'accent que celle-ci met sur la différence et sur la variation. Des fois, elle finit par devenir, comme on peut le voir ci-dessus, une théorie qui sape toutes les catégories de spécification comme "changeantes et instables, comme des positions offertes par des structures discursives, plutôt que par des propriétés d'individus."
Les effets de la déconstruction post-structurale et des théories postmodernistes sur ce concept de sexualité, en tant que concept, ont également ajouté à une sorte d'institutionnalisation des études de la différence dans lesquelles les homosexualités "modernes", "occidentales" deviennent incommensurables par rapport à d'autres homosexualités. Les anciens Grecs sont considérés

comme amoureux des garçons de manière non réciproque, et les rapports homosexuels de cette période comme n'étant *pas* basés tant sur le désir (comme dans l'entendement de la société moderne), mais sur des notions selon lesquelles le plus jeune homme a besoin d'évoluer socialement, alors que l'homme le plus âgé recherche l'intimité intellectuelle que les femmes semblent de toute évidence ne pas avoir.[45] Cela est représenté comme étant différent de notre entendement du "sujet homosexuel moderne" qui est caractérisé par sa volonté de rendre et de s'adonner à des rapports émotionnels et romantiques et qui est également exclusif. L'on pensait que de telles catégories d'individus n'auraient pu exister par le passé, et tout particulièrement dans le contexte clandestin des rassemblements et des activités homosexuelles du tiers-monde opprimé.

Michel Foucault a eu une énorme influence sur notre conception de la sexualité, en tant que concept qui, selon lui, était une invention du dix-neuvième siècle. En fait, Foucault est l'auteur des approches théoriques à l'histoire de la sexualité qui ont été adoptées par les récents travaux critiques. Contrairement à l'approche essentialiste, Foucault écrit :

> Mon objectif n'était pas d'écrire une histoire des comportements et des pratiques sexuelles, de retracer leurs formes successives, leur évolution, et leur dissémination; ou encore d'analyser les idées scientifiques, religieuses ou philosophiques par le biais desquelles ces comportements ont été représentés. Je voulais d'abord me consacrer à cette notion assez récente et banale de "sexualité": garder mes distances par rapport à celle-ci, mettre sa familiarité

entre parenthèses, afin d'analyser le contexte théorique et pratique avec lequel elle a été associée. Le terme lui-même ne fait pas son apparition avant le début du dix-neuvième siècle, un fait qui ne devrait être ni sous-estimé, ni interprété à l'extrême. Il montre toutefois qu'il existe quelque chose autre qu'une simple refonte du vocabulaire, mais évidemment, il ne marque pas l'émergence soudaine de ce à quoi la "sexualité" fait référence." [3]

Mais ces idées de Foucault *ont été* interprétées à l'extrême, parce que l'accent a été mis sur l'idée selon laquelle l'histoire de la sexualité révèle "quelque chose autre qu'une simple refonte du vocabulaire" pour ce qui est de la formation des identités sexuelles et de la connaissance de soi. Alors que, entre temps, le reste de cette idée était négligé, c'est-à-dire que la récente histoire du discours sur la sexualité n'a *pas* "marqué la soudaine émergence de ce à quoi la "sexualité" fait référence."

Et c'est précisément cette répugnance à accepter que le vocabulaire contemporain *peut* être utilisé pour nous informer sur le passé qui prédomine dans la critique contemporaine à laquelle nous faisons allusion. Ce n'est pas en soi l'idée de Foucault selon laquelle le concept de "sexualité" a une courte histoire, mais nous restons sceptique en ce qui concerne la conclusion de Foucault selon laquelle la sexualité a été "conçue comme une constante" *par erreur* (4), ne serait-ce que parce que "ce à quoi la "sexualité" fait référence" est une constante que l'on peut voir facilement, même si cela est de manière imprévue, dans l'étude de cas de l'homosexualité des femmes dans l'Arabie médiévale. Serions-nous en fin de compte peut-être condamnés à donner un nom (un signifiant arbitraire comme le suggère Nietzsche[46]) à ces phénomènes sans nom, bien que ces noms arbitraires fassent référence à des entités permanentes ? Qu'y a-t-il en dessous des échafaudages discursifs de la culture ? Le désir homosexuel des femmes est certainement l'une de ces entités.

Incompréhension de l'homosexualité des femmes au Moyen Orient.

Quand certaines personnes ont appris que nous nous intéressions particulièrement à la civilisation et à la culture islamiques, elles s'attendaient à entendre parler des punitions horribles infligées à ceux qui étaient pris en flagrant délit – décapitations, lapidations, pendaisons, crimes d'honneur : ce genre de choses arrivent bien sûr, mais pas à l'échelle proportionnelle à l'attention que leur accordent les médias occidentaux quand il s'agit de l'homosexualité dans le monde arabe contemporain. Nous sommes d'avis que quelque chose présentée sous l'angle de l'érudition désespérée d'Irshad Manji dans *Musulmane, mais libre* (*The Trouble With Islam*) aurait été bien reçue et aurait satisfait les attentes de la "décadence" des nations musulmanes vivant dans ce qu'elle appelle avec dédain "l'emprise du tribalisme du désert."[47]

Mais notre recherche ne satisfait pas les attentes de ceux qui espéraient qu'elle leur rappelle l'infériorité du Moyen Orient dans le domaine des libertés publiques, d'une façon qui n'a rien à voir avec le rôle impérial de l'Occident dans cette décadence. En fait, en comprenant les cultures islamiques précédentes, ainsi que la variété et l'hétérogénéité des cultures contemporaines par rapport à l'homosexualité des femmes dans la région, on en arrive à une appréciation et une compréhension beaucoup plus profondes du monde arabe, un monde qui, de l'extérieur, apparaît comme répressif, fermé, immuable, mais qui révèle des contradictions dynamiques – des Enfers de résistance et de subversion.

La poésie médiévale sur le sujet de l'homosexualité dans le monde arabe était divisée par les anthologistes de la période en catégorie de censure contre la catégorie des louanges. C'est particulièrement le cas dans les travaux de Tifashi qui sont traduits et figurent en annexe du présent article. Examinons un exemple de la catégorie de la censure :

> Que Dieu te maudisse, infidèle putain [écrit un homme blessé et plein de machisme]
> Comment peux-tu frotter ton pubis contre un autre pubis
> Alors que toute maison ayant un plafond
> Doit avoir un pilier en son milieu ?

Alors qu'une réponse homosexuelle à ce genre de censure avait été formulée en période médiévale, elle n'a survécu que dans la collection de Tifashi et, pendant un moment, dans les Nuits d'Arabie que Richard Burton avait très bien traduit au 19è siècle :

> Un pénis lisse et rond avait été fait/avec un anus lui correspondant / Avait-il été fait pour le bien du con, / il avait la forme d'une hache à main.[48]

Non seulement il y avait une riche collection de documents qui parlaient de désirs homosexuels, mais il semblait que les écrits des savants de la période médiévale sur le sujet portaient sur le caractère inné ou social de l'homosexualité (voir Tifashi et Samaw'uli). Il s'agissait de déterminer si celle-ci était une maladie ou si elle était naturelle, si elle était réversible ou permanente.

Au treizième siècle, Ahmad Ibn Yusuf al-Tifashi (un savant musulman) démontre qu'il n'y avait pas de vue homologue, pas une seule position condamnatoire avancée à chaque niveau de ses anecdotes. Au contraire, si nous nous en remettons à la sensibilité de Tifashi, il y avait une admiration envers certaines des femmes connues sous l'étiquette de copulatrices, mais qui étaient souvent des érudits de l'Islam, ainsi que des musiciens et des artistes, et qui jouaient les rôles de belles esclaves et de femmes libres.

Suite à leur débat sur le caractère inné ou social de l'homosexualité, les savants musulmans de la période médiévale voulaient concevoir des catégories dans l'homosexualité des femmes. Le groupe de lesbiennes semblables aux hommasses modernes était alors connu sous le nom de mutathakirat, bien que certaines d'entre elles étaient probablement des transsexuelles ou, à partir des descriptions de leurs "clitoris" hypertrophiés (qui nous rappellent les études des dix-septième et dix-huitième siècles des tribades occidentales), des intersexuées.49 En fait la silhouette entière de la tribade dans la description de "son" physique est plus convaincante si l'on devait la percevoir comme un "pseudo- hermaphrodite male" – un individu intersexué dont l'anatomie correspond beaucoup plus à la description que le clitoris "lesbien" mythologique que nous associons à la silhouette de la tribade et que nous pourrions maintenant percevoir dans la silhouette de la "mutathakirat". On notera par exemple la description ci-dessous de ces "hommasses" possédant des clitoris hypertrophiés.

> Ils ont dit : Quand elle est excitée, quelque chose sort de sous son estomac qui ressemble au peigne d'une bitte. Cependant, cette description n'est pas exacte : c'est un petit os qui se trouve au dessus de l'entrée du pénis [c'est-à-dire, le vagin], qui ressemble à l'os du nez. Elle monte sur le vagin de son sujet passif et la frotte avec cet os. Ainsi, toutes les deux éprouvent un plus grand plaisir que dans le mariage – le plaisir est plus grand pour la personne active. Quand elle se frotte contre le vagin de la femme passive, alors cet os émerge de façon importante, comme des dents d'enfant, à la seule différence qu'il est long et pas large, et toutes les deux éprouvent un plaisir plus grand que celui que l'on éprouve dans un mariage.

En fait, al-Yemeni avance ici que le peigne d'une bitte "mythologique" (ou le clitoris hypertrophié de la tribade) n'existe pas et affirme au contraire que tous les hommes peuvent découvrir ces parties particulières de l'anatomie (c'est-à-dire le clitoris) : "Et si l'homme visait cet endroit particulier [au dessus de l'entrée du vagin] de la femme avec son pénis, ce dernier apparaîtrait et il verrait de son plaisir et de sa désintégration ce que je mentionne ici."

Parmi ces mutathakirat, il y avait des *femmes* qui n'avaient pas des clitoris élargis, mais qui continuaient à jouer le rôle de ce que l'on appelait "les maniérismes de l'homme" et qui étaient également les amantes d'autres femmes.

> Il y a certaines d'entre elles qui dépassent les autres en intelligence et en déception, et dans leur nature même, il y a beaucoup de caractéristiques semblables à celles

des hommes. Tant et si bien que certaines d'entre elles pourraient ressembler à des hommes dans leurs mouvements et leur façon de parler et leur voix. De telles femmes sont celles qui aiment [à l'opposé d'être aimé], parce qu'elles sont les partenaires actives et ont besoin de quelqu'un qu'elles peuvent chevaucher et ne pas avoir honte de séduire chaque fois qu'elles sont excitées. Il n'est pas convenable pour elles d'avoir des rapports sexuels quand elles ne sont pas excitées. Ceci, ainsi que la difficulté de satisfaire aux plaisirs et aux commandes de l'homme, les conduit à copuler. Le plus grand nombre de celles qui possèdent ces traits est celui des femmes pleines d'esprit, les écrivaines, les lectrices du Coran et les universitaires. Certaines d'entre elles sont attirées par la copulation à cause de l'ampleur des restrictions dont elles font l'objet et qui font qu'elles ont du mal à être seules et en sécurité, sauf avec d'autres femmes. (Samaw'uli)

Célébrées comme les symboles de la visibilité lesbienne, en tant qu'alternative à la tendance générale de la masculinité, subversives et transgresseuses, les hommasses ont fait l'objet de ridicule, ont été accusées de souffrir d'envie du pénis, de vouloir être des hommes, de haïr les hommes et de leur faire concurrence, de re-inventer ou d'imiter un paradigme hétéro - normatif. Il était presque inévitable de constater, pendant que nous rédigions le présent article, le trope de la lesbienne masculine comme facilitant la recherche de tendances. Bien que de nombreuses masculinités de femmes n'aient pas une orientation homosexuelle et que la plupart de ces masculinités qui semblent appartenir aux femmes peuvent être en fait masculines au niveau psychique ou physique, nous pouvons toutefois affirmer, sans peur de nous tromper, qu'il existe de nombreuses hommasses, et qu'une approche culturelle spécifique au trope de la lesbienne masculine ne peut pas nous donner la vraie signification des similarités transhistoriques et transculturelles.

Notre intention, en présentant ce document à la communauté universitaire internationale est de revigorer un débat qui a atteint une sorte d'impasse : si tout est construit par les êtres humains et leurs sociétés respectives, alors sur quel fondement pré linguistique réalisons-nous ces constructions ? Nous espérons que le document présenté en annexe nous aidera à apporter des éléments de réponse à ces questions essentialistes qui ont été négligées à cause de leur apparente complexité.[50]

An Appendix of Texts from the Arabian Middle Ages Concerned with Female Homosexuality

"On the Mention of Grinding and Grindings." In al-Yemeni, Ahmad Bin Mohamad Bin Åli (d. 850). *Rashd al-Labeeb Ila Muåsharat al-habib.* n.c: Thala Lil Tibaåt Wal Nashr, 2002. P123-132.

Grinding is an old trait in women and they find pleasure in it which facilitates the exposure of their secret and their becoming famous for it. He [i.e. Prophet Muhamad] peace be upon him (p.b.u.h) said: "women grinding each other is fornication." The first woman to set grinding was the daughter of Hassan Yamani. She came by Nu'man Bin Al-Muthir and so he took her to his wife Hind. She fell madly in love with her. Hind was the best of the folks of her time, she was completely without excesses. The daughter of Hassan did not cease to deceive her and to extol grinding for her and to say: in the union of two women there is a pleasure that cannot be between the woman and the man. To safeguard herself from scandal and knowing that her appetite could be satisfied without accusation or fear of punishment, they had intercourse (*Ijtama'ata*). Hind found a pleasure that was even greater than the other had described and their amorous desire for each other increased—and it had never been so between women before this.

When the daughter of Hassan died, Hind sat at her grave all the time until people began to use her as an example for their sayings. Al-Farzdak said:

> I was devoted to you in a time that you bestowed kindly
> As Hind was devoted to Hassan Yamani's daughter.

Then after them came Rughum and Najda—they romanced each other and they became famous for their grinding, until Rughum's brother was taunted for his sister's behaviour. So he waited until he came upon them one day as they were having intercourse. Then he killed Najda and took his sister away with him. Rughum began to incite Najda's people to kill her brother and a war erupted between them. This serves as an indication of the greatness of the pleasure they find in grinding, as well as an indication of their preference for grinding over the pleasure with men.

There are two kinds of grinders:

Some of them love grinding but do not hate the penis. Their inclination to grinding and the trials of it occur due to one of four reasons: Perhaps due to the intensity of her sexual dissatisfaction, or the dispensation of an appetite that she cannot find satiation for—this causes her great [masculine] arousal and the rubbing of lips against lips, which brings her satisfaction. This woman can be rescued from doubt as to what is just and extracted from mood to truth by a skilled man who is rich in ways of intercourse and who can offer her various forms of fucking, until she finds one she prefers and which agrees with her appetite, and who then administers it to her. We have seen that when a hen is absent from the rooster's company for too long then she begins to behave like the rooster towards the other hens, and mounts them and crows a cockcrow. However, when she comes by the rooster and hears his crow and learns from him the truth of the mount then she would cease to crow or to mount other hens.

I have seen a woman who became famous for grinding and [masculine] arousal then appeared in her speech, but then she married and left grinding and her attributes became softer.

As for ignorance of the beauty of marriage and overlooking its capacities, then this is also easily demonstrable and the woman is close to returning to what is just. It has been said that a grinder saw the erect penis of a man and so she said:

"There is a pestle like this in the world while I have been knocking at my door with the palm of my hand for twenty years?" Then she left grinding and desired men.

Some resort to this to obviate pregnancy because they hate children and to avoid scandal. In this way such a woman takes up grinding to fulfil her needs. Sometimes a woman would be from her beginning dominated, commanded by a woman to whom she is a subordinate and whose orders she is unable to refuse. Alternatively what she has hated is then made attractive to her, so that when she tastes the pleasures of the act then she wishes to continue in this, and then likes to do this to another in order to give her the pleasure that she has found. The other woman is then as passive during this act as the beardless (*Amrad,* i.e. young man, boy), who when released from the grips of sodomy then is not concerned with anything more than becoming a sodomite.

The second kind:

This is a woman who is masculine (*Mutathakeera*) in appearance and this becomes apparent in her from an early age. She competes with men and resembles them and scorns (haughtily rejects) submitting to them. She rejects being fucked and undermines penises and competes with men over deflowering other women, and she equals the men in jealousy over and protection of women. Finally she fucks the *Amrad* when she becomes erect. They have said: When she is erect something comes out from below her stomach that looks like a cock's comb. However, this description is not accurate: it is a thin bone which is found above the penis-entrance [i.e. vagina], which resembles the nose bone. She climbs up on the vagina of her passive subject and she rubs her with it. When she does this they both feel a pleasure greater than marriage—the pleasure is greater for the active one. When she rubs against the vagina of the woman to whom this is done, then it emerges quite significantly like baby-teeth, except that it is long not wide, and they both find a pleasure greater than that to be found in marriage. And if the man intended that particular place in the woman with his penis then it would appear for him, and he would see from her pleasure and her disintegration what I have here mentioned.

The beardless's (*Amrad's*) anus would be made to bleed when she fucks him. He would then be deluded into thinking that this is something that came out of her vagina—it is rather from the roughness of her hair and the intensity with which she feels herself against him. And the grinder does everything during grinding that the man does in marriage, such as embracing, holding and kissing—as well as grinding on each side and sitting between bent and open legs, which is called *Al-Koori*, and this allows her to access the behind. She only does this when fucking the *Amrad*.

If such a woman fucked and became pregnant, then she does not do this because she craves to fuck men, but she does because a particular man suits her own purposes, and so she desires to have sex with him and no other man.

A grinder wrote to a woman who is afraid of pregnancy (*Mutaqeeya*) saying:

> This is my parchment; I give to you, by my life
> So look at what I have written in it and consider it
> I see nothing ill about you
> You can reveal what I say or veil it…
> For if you see reason in what I say then accept it
> And if not then leave it be.

And come to me consciously and contemplatively so that I can show you a concubine who is no less beautiful than you are, nor inadequate in perfection, whose hair is black as coal and whose bosom is soft and whose breast is firm and whose hips are even more so, and who possesses an elegant waist and who is as hot as a stout bull, eloquent, elegant, cute, seductive, serious and not clumsy. She will show you peaks and how to grind. So take the initiative and truly taste these pleasures and learn that I have spoken honestly about grinding:

> Miserable slit incised by the penis
> Where the pleasure passes and reproach and shame remain

And in any case if the matter was accepted, then this is easier than the other method. This is minimal and that is wasteful. This is concealed and that is forbidden. And I have advised you and trust that you should not be exposed.

The *Mutaqeeya* replied:

> The happy patch came to me
> And by your life I have accepted it
> And understood what you have written and constructed
> And set forth between prose and narrative
> So listen—I have not ignored your advice
> And learn—dearest to my heart—
> That I have not ignored what you said about
> Behaving according to the contract [i.e.marriage]

So I was confused, dear sister—God bless you and raise you in his firmament and protect you—you have denied and not thought, you have attributed and not discerned and offended in what you instigated, and called what I am in shameful and demeaning, and censure and dishonour. You have counted your inclinations reasonable and easy and insignificant and subject for boasting, and you set it forth in proverbs and sayings, and argued for evidence and revealing destination. And then you slipped and called for a matter that I do not deny, like how you deny what I prefer. I will respond to what you have said so that you can learn that what has legitimised handshaking for you has made marriage pleasant for us—and what has made stealth agreeable to you has made embracing agreeable to us. The inkwell is of no use without pens and the filly can only be controlled with hard reins, and palms are the best trees and ripe dates are the prettiest fruit... and the pen is the translator of hearts, and without an axis the wheat-mill wheel cannot turn, and emancipation cannot be got without skewers, and the sail cannot be erected without a pole, and the brush is an instrument used for applying mascara to the eyes, and the oven cannot be used without burning, and further: this slit is for that pestle and this bald head is for that hairless, and this pursuer is for that watch tower and this prostrate flat surface is for that erect scaffold. And I say:

> Tell her, she who recommends grinding
> How desolate is the slit against slit
> There was comfort[51] for her in the penis
> But she has deviated from the truth

I frankly speak of your excuse and I am not indignant with you because you tried to shame what you don't know and you have proscribed what you have not tried. No one who hasn't tasted it, knows the worth of honey, and whomsoever has yet to smell musk does not know its glory. And if what you have proscribed was not amongst the greatest pleasures among girls, then a woman would never return to that hardness after labour or to that habit after giving birth. As for the man, he works hard for what he possesses on his wedding day. Consider what happens to those orphan (male) lovers who come forward, because he (the groom) has invited them without thinking—some who lost their family, some who killed themselves out of grief and some who died from heartbreak and pining... do you see them love passionately so that they can be miserly or seclude themselves to kill?

Impossible! They have tasted so they have prohibited and veiled and thus burned and tasted and thus yearned and looked and thus broken their fast[52] and romanced and then burned. And so they ran between madness and infatuation, between slenderness and feebleness, and winging and whining, and increased their insistence for the sake of that need, and lengthened the struggle to feel the pleasure in pleasure, until strangely enough the people of fire boast proudly of firewood, and you offer me a concubine and invite me to her and I teach you what virtue I have over her, and these things can't be known by description but by discovery. So if you want to discover this with a penis between your lips then I have an *Amrad* for you—of good constitution and pleasant countenance, with charming eyelids and of many talents, who is appetising to the mind and who has temples like those of a bride and his cheek is as soft as yours and his body is as light as yours.

> He is of excellent beauty and melodious of voice
> Laudable for his aim, extremely polite
> With a sharp face and a pure mouth
> And a pleasing countenance and a graceful body
> Is the generous type and craves intercourse
> Quite attentive to what you want of him
> Pleasing to fuck, of little dispute and good humour

> Of elegant constitution and rich in speech
> Like the full moon witty and sensual
> Strong bold compassionate jealous
> But in possession of a scorching penis
> He fucks without trouble
> And follows that with five more turns immediately
> So welcome to this and grinding obliteration to that
> Do not approach grinding which is bad for a creature
> And come to me without deviating
> And let me arrange a meeting between you.

Sister we have not assaulted you but offered you as you offered us and approached you as you approached us, so if you want this it is between your hands and if you prefer that then good day to you.

A *Mutaqeeya* gave a citrus fruit as a present to a grinder, which has inside it the appearance of the vagina, naturally, and she wrote these verses:

> When I perused this I said that the citrus tree
> Was more entitled to it than humankind
> A stupendous vagina, as though seared by fire
> That comes between the legs of a concubine
> More splendid than the moon—
> Yellow, sedating, soft
> Born of seaweed and trees.

The grinder replied:

> I have been given a citrus fruit that emits a fragrance
> That the ambergris emits

> And this increases its splendour and adorns it for me
> Something of hers free from the male incursion
> If something else resembled it better
> Then God would not have put it like a sculpture on the trees.

[lacuna]

A *Mutaqeeya* sketched a male slave lifting the legs of a woman he was fucking and sent it to a grinder with the following comment:

> This, by your life, is my condition
> I have naught to do with grinding
> This shoots the heart in an instant, like arrows,
> having a brow like darkness and a countenance like the moon
> And a figure like a reed that glows with evenness
>
> For that is my intimacy and enticement
> For which I would lay down my life and fortune.
> Since this might burden you,
> My deed does not enrich me.

So the grinder sketched her a picture of a concubine grinding her and sent it to the *Mutaqeeya* and she wrote alongside it:

> But my vagina succeeds and glimmers between a cheek and a freckle
> Like a dot of musk swinging above the crescent
> Revealing a pure mouth, smiling like pearls
> In which there is a savoury saliva
> Instantly sweet to the taste

> And a fine neck as beautiful as the gazelle's
>
> From what I have seen of her beauty—
> And O how much have I seen!—
> I say glory to whomever moulded beauty from clay
> To create a perfect creature made of beauty
> I came to sip from her and her extreme thirst is at a well
>
> If that is prohibited (*Haram*) then this is not lawful (*Halal*).

And Abu Nuwas has said:

> There is no meaning to grinding that I know of,
> Because it is fats rubbed by fats
> There is nothing in naked friction
> Until the baldhead enters.

He also said:

> God has shamed the grindings of saffron stigmas
> They have incited a war without weapons
> except the clanging of shield against shield

And of what I have said on this:

> They were confused by her grinding and then said:
> What pleasure is there in having straits within straits?
> I said but her miserable vagina is sick,
> For it is being given the counterfeit of marriage.

Al Jaheth (c. 860) quotes Muthana Bin Zuhair. Cited in Saåeedi, Samir. *Asil al-Aeela al-Arabiya Wa Anwa al Jawaz al-Qadeema 'ind al-Arab.* **Beirut: Dar al Multaqa, 2000. P157-158.**

Muthana Bin Zuhair said:

I have never seen anything in man and woman that I haven't seen in the male and female pigeon.

I have seen a pigeon who did not want anyone besides her male mate in the same way that a woman wants no one besides her husband and master. And I have seen a pigeon who does not forbid any male, as I have seen a woman who does not deter the touching hand. I have seen female pigeons who do not show their depravity until after much rejection and a great deal of insistence. And I have seen it show depravity to the first male who chooses her and I have seen women of that sort too.

I have seen a pigeon who has a mate (husband) while she allows another male access—I have seen this in women too. I have see one flirt with a male other than her mate, whilst her mate was watching, and I have seen one who won't do this unless her husband flies or flaps his wings.

I have seen a female pigeon who mounts male pigeons and one who mounts another female one. I have seen pigeons who mount nothing besides other female pigeons and I have seen one who mounts female ones but does not allow them to mount her. I have seen a male who mounts one who then mounts him in return. I have seen a female pigeon who feigns masculinity (maleness) and who does not allow another to mount her. I have seen all of these kinds in grinders—feminine and masculine ones—and also amongst men who are sodomites.[53]

Among men there are those who do not want women and amongst women those who do not want men...By God I have seen a male pigeon who would mount whatever he finds in his way without ever marrying. I have seen a female pigeon who gave access to any one wanting her, male or female....

From *Al-Aghani* Al-Asfahani, Abu Faraj (c. 972). Hypertext available from http://www.alwaraq.net P1352 & P1905.

Abu Aisha used to fancy a woman (who worked as a professional mourner) of beauty and goodness, who was called Sada—Abi Fadel also fancied her, and she was their superior. Then Abu Aatiha accused her of loving women and he said on that occasion:

> Hey you dignitaries of grinding in the west and east
> Wake up for fucking is more satisfying than grinding
> Wake up because bread is craved with food
> And it cannot be softened in the throat by bread
> I see you trying to patch holes with holes
> And what kind of wit would try to patch a hole with another one?
> And is the hammer of any use without its handle
> If it is needed one day for knocking?

[The story is retold with minor variation on page 1717 of the hypertext.]

***

Al-Ma'mun was sitting with a cup in his hand when Bathal[54] began to sing the song:

> I see nothing more delectable than the promise

But she sang it:

> I see nothing more delectable than grinding.

Al-Ma'mun placed his cup down and turned to her and said: Of course there is, Bathal: fucking is better than grinding. So she became embarrassed and feared his wrath but he picked up his cup again and said: finish the song and add:

> I come to her when the slanderer is unaware
> With a visit to a house empty of visitors except me
> With a cry during the meeting and then a pause
> And all these things are more delectable to me than dwelling [there].

From *Al-Muhalla* by Ibn Hazm Al-Andalusi (d. 1064). Hypertext available from http://www.alwaraq.net P2232.

Mohamad's father, God rest his soul, said: "People disagreed over grinding. One denomination said that 'you whip each one of them with one hundred lashes.' As Ibn Shihab has said: 'I have noticed that our learned men have said that a woman who has sex with another woman through the inner thigh and the like, should be whipped one hundred lashes—the doer and the done to.'

"Some denominations licensed it—as Ibn Jareeh has told me about Al-Hassan Bassri who did not see the woman inserting anything as wretched—simply that she was seeking refuge from scandal (*Satr*), and this way she can do it without committing fornication.

"Others have said that it is forbidden, without exception. Mohamad's father, God bless his soul, has said: 'So when they disagreed—as we have already mentioned—we were obliged to look into this. So we looked into what Zahri has said and we found no legitimacy in it. Zahri said: 'As the people of Lot made the act (of sodomy) at the upper limit of fornication, then by the same token this [grinding] is at the lower limit of fornication. So it is the least act of fornication.'

"The father of Mohamad said, God rest his soul: 'And this measure is an obligation to whoever made the act of Lot's people punishable by stoning, because [as they say] it is greater than fornication, then they have no way out of this but to make grinding also greater than fornication, so they should make the act also punishable by stoning, as they must do with the act of Lot's people, since both matters are deviancies in the genitals which cannot be permitted at all.'

"But people are not good at judgement and do not know how to follow guidance and do not know how to reject hearsay and to adhere to their evidence-based analysis, and they do not rely on texts, and they have said here: 'that Al-Zahri knew the original followers [of the prophet, p.b.u.h], and that he was relating this information from them, but we don't know where he begot his prohibition.' So they apply what he has said if it agrees with their tradition.

"Mohamad's father, God rest his soul, said: 'As for us, the measure [of equating fornication with homosexual acts] is false.

Someone's opinion should not be followed without the messenger of God (p.b.u.h), and grinding and the "inner thigh activity" are not fornication. If they are not fornication then they are not to be treated as such. No one has a right to swear by their opinion—setting the limits of this however he likes. This matter goes back to the limits set by Almighty God who has set laws in religion for what he does not permit, and he has said: 'Whomsoever transgresses the limits set by God is being unfair to himself.'

"And whomsoever supports [Zahri's] poor excuse, has gone too far in error and has made tradition triumphant. The father of Mohammad, God rest his soul, has said: 'and if something like Zahri's saying did not come to be said in the Quran, or set in a correct law, then preaching the limits is prohibited, because there are no limits set originally.'

"They have mentioned that the prophet (p.b.u.h) said: 'grinding is fornication between women.' But this is not correct because it comes as a fragment—and it is weak—and it is related by Wathala and Makhool who are not connected [to the original company of the prophet]. But if this was true, it still does not contain instruction on judging acts according to limits, because he (p.b.u.h) has shown in *hadith Aslamy* what the demarcations of fornication are—and that is a man coming to a woman unlawfully, in a manner that is permitted to his parents but not him. And he told us (p.b.u.h) that members fornicate and the genitals make this either true or false, so there is no fornication between a man and a woman except through the penis being inside the vagina. And this saying should deter those who claim that the act of Lot's people is at the upper limit of fornication. They do not have an authentic text to support this and if they found some such text then they would tyrannize and oppress.

"So this claim is disproved by one sentence.

"Then we looked into what Hassan said about permitting this and we found fault, because God Almighty says: 'Those who expose their genitals to anyone besides their spouses are not keeping their faith and are transgressing.' And this is true given the guidance in the Quran and the *Ijma'a* that a woman is prohibited from being seen by her *Mahram*.[55] God Almighty, however, unveiled [the head only of] the wives of Mohamad before their slaves and their close female relations.

"It is true, however, that the slave can also be entrusted as a *Mahram* by his master; therefore, if the woman displayed her genitals to anyone besides her husband then she is not guarding it and she has disobeyed God Almighty by doing this. It has also been truthfully said that her skin is not permitted to anyone besides her husband, so if she displays her skin to a woman, or a man who is not her husband, then she has acted unlawfully.

"We have also related that… the messenger (p.b.u.h.) has said: 'A man does not look at another man's genitals and the woman does not look at another woman's, and the man does not come to (*yafud*) another man in one blanket, and the woman does not come to another woman in one blanket. Abd Allah Bin Massud said: 'The messenger of God (p.b.u.h) put an end to a woman embracing[56] another woman under one blanket—in case she describes her to her own husband thus making him virtually able to see her.'

"Ibn Abbas has said: 'The messenger of God (p.b.u.h.) has damned men who try to resemble women and women who try to resemble men.'

"The father of Mohamad has said: 'These texts are very intent on forbidding sexual contact (*Mubashara*) between men and women among themselves, and whoever engages in such activity is disobeying God Almighty, and if this sexual contact was made with the genitals then this is even more unlawful and a double insubordination. If the woman inserts anything in her vagina that she is not permitted to insert, such as her husband's genitals or whatever she needs during menstruation, then she is not guarding it, and if she does not guard it then she is increasingly insubordinate. Therefore Hassan's saying is erroneous."

"The reason for some women's preference for grinding." In al-Samaw'uli, Abu Nasr bin Yahya bin Åbbas al-Maghribi (d. 1180). *Kitab Nuzhat al-Ashab fi Muåsharat al-Ahbab.* **Chapters 6-8. P13-17. Edited and compiled from original manuscripts by Taher haddad. PhD. Diss., Friedrich Aleksander University, n.d. P3-29.**[57]

Some women prefer grinding because they are slow at cumming, due to the coldness of their womb or the coldness or scarcity of their fluid. For if they had intercourse they would be beaten to cumming and thus they rise without having achieved their need. Whenever the man separates from one such woman and where the flame of her sexual appetite is ablaze then she would go so far as to bring down a horse on her, if she could. That is, if nothing stops her and women who are slow at cumming have little to stop them. Alternatively, she would resort to a female lover whom she chooses or a eunuch who will be at her disposal. Should a woman with this trait come by a man who is slow at cumming then he would distract her from grinding and turn her away from it.

Some women develop a preference for grinding as a result of the shortness of their wombs or a result of the great length of their (male) partner's device. This causes such women pain during intercourse and does not rouse their appetites, thus, nothing suits them except men with small devices.

If a woman who is quick at cumming comes across a man who is slow at doing so then, no sooner does he enter her, does she cum. If her fluid reaches his penis then this cools it and slows his cumming even more—if he continues on inside her then she might cum a second time. Should her mood not be so inclined, then she would (after the second cumming) have no desire to do anything except lie motionless and ease the matter for her womb. At such time the man would be at the peak of his going to and fro and at the most extreme of his carefulness as he nears cumming—so she sighs and becomes bored and restless and thus her desire for men weakens. As a result she begins to grind. If she comes across a man who is quick at cumming then he would be suitable for her.

Some women have deficiencies or illnesses in their wombs and as a result intercourse causes them pain. These women compensate by grinding and become satisfied with it.

There are some women whose problem lies in wanting to kiss a mouth that is not roughened by a beard and wanting to press their cheeks against a soft cheek. If one such woman managed to find a young unbearded man (*amrad*) then she would attain her satisfaction. Alternatively she would compensate with a girl[58] grinder where she can be choosy about her beauty. This is better for her [to be able to choose whom she likes] than to be warranted to the thick blackness [i.e. beard] that she cannot bear. So what think you of this low-life gathering at the place of such a morally venomous snake?

It has been said that A'anan Natafi's concubine used to fancy a young son of one of the merchants. She would try to get his attention but he would not acknowledge her and she would write to him but he would not reply—so she forgot him. After some time she came by him accidentally. He had grown a beard and he was pleased to see her and tried to speak to her. She ignored him and went to her house and wrote to him:

> O how you were desired for the softness of your face—
> The temperance of your youth... and you were granted purity
> And now time has veiled you with a beard
> Which, for my sake, is best plucked.
> You were a face that came and went
> And now, however you turn your face, it is a backside.

And for some of them who share this opinion:

> You are a full moon that has been aggrieved by the eclipse
> From whose darkness there is no escape.

And for some:

> O how you came to be desired for the softness of your face
> The temperance of youth on your hairless visage
> Now a beard has appeared on your cheek and has
> Taken your beauty and given you a donkey's reins
> Like the delectable juice freshly fermented which becomes sour vinegar

There are some of them who exceed others in intelligence and deception and in their nature there is much that resembles men. So much so that one of them might resemble men in her movements and her speech and her voice. Such a woman is a lover[59] because she is the active partner and so she needs someone she can be on top of and not be ashamed to seduce every time her appetite is roused. It does not suit her to have intercourse at the time when her appetite is dormant. So this, together with the difficulty in cumming under the pleasures and command of the man, leads her to grinding. The greatest number of those who possess these traits are among the witty women, and the writers and the Quranic readers[60] and the scholars. Some of them are drawn to grinding due to the intensity of restriction imposed on them, where they are unable to be alone safely and privately except with other women.

And some women whose womb is dominated by coldness, find pleasure in the heated friction and there is no pleasure like it in intercourse, because the friction of the two bodies causes high temperatures. The act then heats up the fluid channels which open up and draw the fluid out.

On grinding:

Hey you grinders of east and west
Wake up for fucking is better than grinding
Wake up because bread is craved with food
And it cannot be softened in the throat by bread
I see you trying to patch holes with holes
And what kind of wit would try to patch a hole with another?

From *Nihayat Al-Arb Fi Funoon al-Adab* by Al-Nuwayri (c. 1241). Hypertext available at http://www.alwaraq.net **P1323.**

Kassi said that Kaáb said: The people of Rus were many and they built a city forty miles long, and they named it Rassan, which was also the name of their king. They lived a long time in their country worshipping God Almighty, the way he ought to be worshipped, and then they deviated from this and worshipped statues, and they began to practice sodomizing women and swapping them. Every man would send his woman to another. This became unbearable for the women, and so the devil came to them as a woman and taught them grinding and so they did it. And they are the first people to sodomize women and whose women grinded each other. These uglinesses spread amongst them.

"On the Literature of Grinders and their Grinding." In Tifashi, Ahmad Ibn Yusuf. *Nuzhat Al-Albab Fima La Yujad Fi Kitab* (c.1250). Reproduced in a modern edition by Jamal Juma'a, ed. London: Riaad Al-Rayyes, 1992. P235-247. This and subsequent translations are my own.

Doctors noted that the origin of this illness was within women's physical constitution, and then there was disagreement over the reason for this. Some of them noted that the nature of the womb was inverted and that the woman's womb was congenitally the same as the male member, no difference between them except that the male member is evident from the outside and is narrow, while the woman's womb, which is inverted within, is broad. They noted that if the male member became erect inside the woman's womb he blocked it from all sides lengthwise and width-wise. And for this reason the woman and man find the touching and union of the two members pleasurable.

They said: Just as the male's member varies in length and shortness, so it is with the woman's womb. So if the dimensions of the woman's womb were suited to that of the penis, then she would like him, and if it was not suited to her then she would hate him.

For example: Should the length of her womb be short and the man's member long, then she would be harmed by it and hate men and like grinders. Or should he possess a short penis and where her womb is long, then she could not be satisfied except by those with a very long device.

Wherever [female homosexual] grinding[61] activity is caused by a shortness in the womb, then hatred of men is continuous for its owner, for whom this ailment is a constant companion.

***

And it has been said that Son of Massoyeh said:

"I read in the old books that grinding is created when the breast feeder eats celery and watercress and sweet clover,[62] if she consumes too much of these things and then breastfeeds, she then transfers the adverse effects of this to the labia of the infant. For then itchiness is created and this illness is woman's harlotry because, in the man, this is an itchiness that appears in the anus.

Or perhaps grinding was a kind of attachment to a habit of using concubines, from an early age for this, where they mature on it and they continue to crave it. In the same way as licentiousness, as we will reveal later, whenever grinding is self-generated[63] then it is easily soluble, easily transferable, but when it is due to physical constitution, then it is difficult to recover from and is far from accepting treatment, as we have noted.

***

Some wise men have said:

"Grinding is a natural appetite that occurs between the labia, that is concave like an inverted boil out of which vapours are generated. These increase and consequently heat is generated as well as itchiness in the hair floccules of the labia. This does not go away or cool except with the grinding and the going (or coming) down on her from another woman. And if this happens then the itchiness will cool and be extinguished, because the woman's water (fluid), that comes from grinding is cold, whereas the one that comes from the man is hot, and for this reason she does not benefit except from the woman's water (fluid) which can only be extracted by grinding.[64]

***

And I know that this matter is known among its masters as wit[65] and by this name they are called, meaning, they call themselves: The witty ones. So if they said that so and so is "witty" then it becomes known amongst them that she is a grinder. And they romance each other like men, but more intensely: one of them will spend money on the other in the same way that a man does on his lover, but much more, until the spending is exaggerated to hundreds and thousands.

I witnessed one woman of them in Morocco. She had a great deal of money and an extensive estate, so she spent a great deal of jewellery-money on her lover. So when she ran out of this and people began to reproach and blame her exceedingly, she conceded to her lover the entire estate, which came to about five thousand dinars.

***

Moreover they use a lot of fragrance/perfume beyond what is usual, and the cleanness of their clothes is more than is characteristic, and as for furniture, food and devices,[66] of these they have better and more beautiful things than capability can attain or place and time contain.

***

And about their condition:

That the lover be on top and the loved one below except if the lover is thin and the loved one robust. In such a case the thin one is placed below and the robust one on top, so that the heaviness of her waist is nearer to the friction/grinding, as it (the heavy waist) is better suited to fulfilling that purpose.

***

A description of what they do:

That the lower one sleeps on her back and extends one thigh and leg and embraces the other revealing her vulva, leaning to one side. And then comes the top one and hugs the elevated thigh and places one of her lips on the lips of the lower one and grinds (rubs) to and fro at the length of the body, up and down and for this reason they liken it to the grinding of saffron because similarly, saffron is difficult to access.

And if she had begun by placing her right lip then she would rub it for an hour and then transfer the rubbing to the left one, until the couple[67] satisfy their carnality. As for placing both lips atop the other lips, this is not useful for them nor is it pleasurable and the reason for this is because the place of pleasure remains empty of an occupant, and perhaps they facilitate their activity by applying ben-oil ointment.

Moreover, the most practised of their conditions and the most variant, which are also necessary and indispensable, are the rules of "Cuteness" and the expertise in moaning and groaning and the mastering of the trade of sweet talk that arouses the appetite at the time. They even discuss this and teach it and expend desirables on women who are wise in it, so that they can teach it to the ones who are not good at it.

***

It has been said of the urban[68] Huba, who was the most renowned of grinders, that she said to her daughter: "you have to groan well during the banging (to and fro) and know that I let out a scream in the desert once that so startled Othman bin Affan's camels, God bless him, they haven't managed to re-collect them to this day."

***

One of the scholars in Damascus engaged me in conversation and said: "one of the highest-ranking Egyptian judges told me:

"'I went out one night to the cemetery, and this cemetery was for the use of the Egyptian householders where they met their female friends. It is a place where women gather every week, so they are not forbidden to meet there and spend the night or use it as a dwelling. Within the cemetery they have built residences, on which a considerable sum of money has been spent," he said. "So I decided that I would leave my home with the intention of staying there with my family, supplying myself with whatever I needed for sleep as well as food and hay for the mule and so on. I closed the door to my house and darkness progressed with its lamp and I traversed on my own, riding the mule, until the hour became late and I arrived at the cemetery after sunset and at the onset of darkness. And as I was walking amongst the graves, in a remote place in one of the corners of the cemetery, I heard, in one of the graves, a moaning and groaning and a kind of panting that strips the mind and steals the heart. I had never heard anything like it and I didn't think anyone did it as such: with measured movements and natural rhythms and sayings of internal rhyme that cause one to forget the melody of strings and render the mistresses of the flute invisible.

'And so I steered my mule to the wall of the tomb and then I climbed up and looked in, to find two women. The one on the bottom was a Turkish concubine who was more beautiful than the full moon and more balanced than the branch. She was white, soft and busty, and on top of her there was a short woman, robust, nice looking, clean clothes, except she didn't look like the one below her, as she grinded her and treated her to this talk. Meanwhile, the woman below replied a little inadequately as though she was learning from her.[69]

'And so when I saw this I could not hold myself together and I yelled out at them and said: "Rise, God damn you!" And I rode towards the tomb with the intention of locking them in, and then calling on passers-by to discipline them. By the time I was at the door, the one who was on top had got up, and the bottom one had begun to get up, and so she said to her: "Stay where you are." And so she remained lying on her back and then uncovered her belly and navel and her chest, by removing a blue robe that was on her, and there appeared a chest like marble, and breasts like pomegranates, and a belly like a mound of snow, in which the naval appeared as a fat vial that has crystallized into a hot white curd, tinged with redness. I had never seen anything with its greatness or pureness. And then she said to me:

'"Damn you, you beast, you oppressor, have you ever seen anything like this?" So I said to her: "By God no." She said to me: "Here is before you a rare feast that God has prepared for you, so go on your way."

'He said: When I saw and heard this I was stripped of reason and morality and I could not control myself, so I said to her: "Damn you, I have this mule." She said: "So I'll hold it for you."

'He said: I alighted, and as God is my witness, I was going against my nature in doing this, and then I gave her the reins and the whip and I entered the tomb. I undid the flag's knot[70] and placed it on my leg and then I loosened my pants and threw the end of my pallium over my shoulder, and I inserted my hand and removed my tail.[71] I drew near the concubine and I bent over her and when I brought the head of my penis to the lips and found their softness and warmth, I did not feel anything other than the hooves of my mule departing and the woman yelling: "I've let go of the mule."

'So I got up, devoid of reason and sensibility, and I went outside, and there was the mule departing among the graves in the gathering darkness. Since I lost sight of him, I did not know where he went, but I ran after him in that condition: member erect, pants undone, the flags on the top of my feet, my pallium tangled up—getting up one minute and falling again at another.

'And the mule continued in his early departure and I continued to run after him, and moreover the damned woman, when she had let him go, struck him on his waist with the whip, so the mule began to move towards anyone who approached him and to kick at them with his heels. I ran after him in a condition which if it had only been a sketch on paper would have caused the melancholic much laughter and stopped those in a hurry, so how much funnier would it have been to see in reality!

'And it so happened that the mule had passed his feeding time, and he was better at finding his way to the city than the sand grouse, and he continued to run and I to run after him, unable to catch him, and so he would disappear in the darkness or someone would find him and ride him and then I could see nothing more than dust. And I came across some people and they saw me in that condition and they spoke to me, but I was out of my mind because of what happened to me as a result of that whoresome woman's amusement—because when I ran after that mule I heard their laughter behind me and she yelling out to me: "Come back, judge! Come on, where are you going?" And the others laughed in my face as I was running.

'The mule did not stop until he put his head through the house door, and there I was met by many people, in that same scene, some who knew me, and some who didn't.'"

***

One of the wise men said to one of the brazen-faced, when a mention of grinding was made: "By God I crave to know how women fuck/grind each other." He said: "If you like that, then go inside your house bit by bit [a little bit at a time]."

***

In Praise of Grinding and its Admonition
They said:
Women go to it for fear of pregnancy and ugliness.

***

I conversed with Ismael bin Mohammed, who said: "Koraisha, the pimp, conversed with me. She said:

'"I said to a concubine once: so and so loves you. She said, 'I love him too,' so I said: 'Why don't you visit him?' 'For fear of us becoming three.'"

***

And it was said to a man: "your woman grinds." He said: "If she excuses me of what causes weaning in the belly, then let her do whatever she likes."[72]

And it was said to Mazeed: "Your wife grinds." He said, "Yes, I ordered her to do so" and so it was said "Why?" He said: "because it is softer on her lips, and purer to the opening of her labia, and more proper, should the penis be presented to her that she should know its grace."

***

Warda, the grinder, said:

"We accompany the grinders; any one of us can be joined with one who is white, soft, flirtatious, succulent, tender-skinned as though she is a bamboo stalk, with a mouth like daisies, and ringlets like dark beads, and a cheek like anemone or the apples of Lebanon, and a breast like pomegranates, and a stomach with four folds, and a vagina that conceals fire, with two lips that are coarser than the Israelite's cow, and a hunch like the hump of Thamood's camel, and a behind as though it is the fat-tail of Ishmael's sheep, in the colour of ivory, and with the softness of a silken garment, shaved and perfumed, anointed with musk and saffron as though it is king Anushurwan in the midst of the palace, where temples are decorated with small ringlets, and throats are ornamented with pearls and hyacinth and Yemeni slips and Egyptian headscarfs.

"So we isolate ourselves with them with impassioned reproaches and a benevolent tone, and charming eyelids that strip the heart of its blackness. So that if our chests are superimposed upon each other, and throats embrace throats and lips are fitted to lips, and each of them quivers against the other, then the breathing heightens and the senses are preoccupied and fever is raised from the head, and then there would be no measure of this left, as you look for erotic moves and illusory consciences and instinctual drives and amorous civility, between sucking and pinching, and going to and fro, and inhalation and sighing and moaning and murmuring and groaning, that should the people of Malta hear, they would call out: it's the bugle![73] With raising and placing and winking and suggesting, and embracing and smelling and consistency and kisses, and pleasure taken in the work, and the turning of sides without worry....

All this with a royal literature and fragrant moaning, so that if unloading came and the decorations decreased, you smell like the breeze of flowers in March and the fragrances of wine in a bottle of alcohol, and you look to the shaking of the ben-oil tree branch in the rain. For if the philosophers looked at what we are in, it would confuse them, while the masters of romance and delights would have been caused to fly.

***

Regulations/Laws in this

Some of them have said:
One of the strangest things in her time
And God is neither forgetful nor a breaker of promises

That when two stay overnight together
That a third would come between them.

Another:

I drank wine for love of romance/courtship
And I inclined to grinding for fear of pregnancy
So I had sex in remoteness, with my lover
And I exceeded the men in the proficiency of the work
If my grinding was convincing then it made me rich and caused me to reject the man

Another:

How much have we grinded sister, ninety pilgrimages
More delightful and invisible than the entries of the penis head,[74] and than
A pregnancy that pleases the enemy and worse than that, the reproaches
Of the censurers
And we are not limited in grinding,
Like in fornication, even though it is more
Delicious to the inclined.

***

Another:

I was convinced by my lover and rejected a penis
Whose disadvantages in that fate, shame us.

If it is said that I became pregnant, then annihilation of
Illegitimate children narrows my chest

So what excuse for the parents would I give?
For fornication has broken
The ropes of my back.

Denouncement of Grinding

Hashima spoke. She said:

"A Woman wrote to a lover of hers who had married and ceased to see her:

'My sister if everyone who saw a walking stick then started walking on it, because of whatever weakness he had, and benefited from it, then I would have excused you for not being able to walk except with a stick. But there is no admiration for your leaving what is in your nature, in order to walk in the darkness,[75] because this impoverishes your body.'

"So she wrote her a reply: 'My sister, I used to enjoy the beating of the drum before I enjoyed the sound of the flutes. So when I heard it, something in my heart knotted up that nothing except death can resolve. So make it easy on yourself, by not making my fate your business, because it has become easier on me, because of the privilege that I now have in my hands.'"

***

And another wrote to a lover of hers who had tasted a man and accompanied him: "If the Muezzin never came down from the Mimbar, then no one would pray in the dwelling. So what is this admiration for a bucket that has been dipped in a thousand wells and then became yours, when its edges are dented and its rope is eroding? If you return to what is fair, then you will find that walking in the garden is easier than walking the arduous mountain road."

So she wrote a reply: "My sister, I used to eat onion without knowing the taste of damask rose, and radish. So when I ate them I swore that I would eat nothing else besides. No, [I swear] by your life, you did not come into my house ever, so expunge my love from your heart, because I have put, in place of your love, something that will only come out with breath [spirit]."

***

And it was said to a grinder who married: "How was your night, last night?" She said: "I used to crave meat and I was not satiated until last night."

***

And a grinder looked on a man with a large penis and she said: "There is a pounder such as this in the world and I beat my clothes with my hand? This won't be forever." And so she married.

The Laws In This

God has damned the grindings of saffron stigmas[76]
Because they have exposed[77] the fires of humans
They have aroused a war without stabbing
Only the clanging of shield against shield

***

To another:

For by God, should my penis come by you
In the darkness between dawn and sunrise, at the time of Suhoor[78]
Then you would learn that all grinding is false
And that the truth is in the tip of the penis.

***

Another:

God damn you, you unfaithful whore
How do you rub your pubis with another pubis
When every house that is covered by a ceiling
Must have a pillar in the middle of it.

***

Another:

Hey you—dignitaries[79] of grinding in west and east
Wake up—for fucking is better than grinding
Wake up—because food[80] is craved with bread
And bread cannot be softened in the throat by bread

If they were to patch holes in the same manner
Then what kind of wit would patch a hole with a hole?
And is the hammer of any use without its stick[81]
If it was needed one day for hammering?

***

Another:

Leave the grinding that has exhausted you falsely
For no grinder is satisfied by grinding
And there is beneath you the tip of a knob that thickens and lengthens
With which you could do whatever you like in terms of pounding and thinning out.
When, on your life, have you ever seen an attempt to fill a hole with a hole?

Another:

Say to whoever fancies grinding, which God has prohibited because there is no good in it:

You have erred, you who are full of virtue, if you put Isaac in place of Zabeer.[82]

From *Diwan Al-Sababa* by Ibn Abi Hajala (c. 1421). Hypertext available from http://www.alwaraq.net P87.

The *Amrad* are preoccupied with promiscuity
and the people's women are preoccupied with grinding.
Every sex is unto itself sufficient
And such is the solace to the kinsfolk of wantonness.

***

The following is a polite response to a woman who deserves to have it said, if only to be fair to her:

> Enamoured of grinding
> You have been crying over it with every eye
>
> [Lacuna]

It has been told that a man entered a house where he found two women grinding. So the one on top pulled him and put him in her place, and he said that this is a matter that requires ropes and men.

Our Sheik Zein Addin Ibn Al-Wardi recited a poem about women of our time:

> Say to whoever fancies grinding
> Which the Good God has prohibited
> You err perfectly good lady
> When you put Isaac in place of Zabeer.

And another said:

> Say to her who grinds, what are you grinding for?
> Nothing satisfies your burning thirst
> Except these poor, bald, shaven saddlebags.

From *Kanz Al-Umal* by Al-Mutqee Al-Hindi (c.1597). Hypertext available at http://www.alwaraq.net **P675.**

From Wathala: Women grinding each other is fornication.

There are at least ten reasons for Lot's people's annihilation: Men having sex with each other, and their throwing of arrows and oars, and their playing with pigeons and beating of drums, for their drinking of alcohol, and cutting their beards and having long moustaches, for their whistling and wearing silk, and for women having sex with each other. Taken from Ibn Askar from Al-Hassan.

Women cannot marry each other, and a woman cannot marry herself, except the fornicator: she marries herself. Taken from Abi Hurreira.

From *Salwat Al-Ahzan lil Ijtinab 'an Mujalasat al-Ahdath wal Niswan* by al-Mashtoolee (c. 1787) Hypertext available from http://www.alwaraq.net P49.

Women having sex with each other is one of the major transgressions. Wathila Bin Al-Aska said: The messenger of God (p.b.u.h) said: "Grinding is women fornicating together."

He also said, p.b.u.h: "Female genitals on each other are like male genitals on female ones." He also said: "Women cannot have sex with each other without fornicating."[83]

He also said: "And thirdly God does not accept their doxology 'there is no God but Allah'—the rider and the ridden upon, whether they are a male or female couple."

And Ali said, God bless him: "If men became satisfied with men and women by women, there will be disfigurement and bombardment and hammering from the heavens." And Atta, citing Abi Hurreira, God bless him: "The messenger of God (p.b.u.h) said: 'There comes a time when people marry male slaves and not women and they alternate between male slaves and women.' This sin is reinforced whenever the doer is not deterred from it."

Al Sheik Taki Addin Al-Hassani, God rest his soul, said in his explication of Abi Sjuja's book: "Women grinding each other is prohibited and they are reprehended for this because it is an unlawful act."

And the judge Abu Al-Tayib, God rest his soul, said: "This sin is the same as the sin of fornication on the strength of his saying (p.b.u.h): 'If a woman had sex with another woman then they are fornicators.' Also this is apparent when we are told that if a woman mounted another woman then God commands an angel to dress her in seventy garments and seventy armours of fire."

Effeminacy in Men and what it Entails.

The meaning of effeminacy: The man attempts to resemble woman in his speech and dress and all other demeanours. This is one of the greatest sins which calls for damnation—not only for the man's attempt to resemble a woman but for the woman's attempt to resemble man. Ibn Abbas, God bless him, had said: "The messenger of God (p.b.u.h) has damned effeminate men and man-acting (masculine) women." And this is a true *hadith*. Abu Hurreira, God bless him, has said that "the messenger of God (p.b.u.h) has damned the men who wear women's clothes and the women who wear men's clothes."

From *Wafi Bil Wafiyat* by Al-Safadi (d. 1787). Hypertext available from http://www.alwaraq.net **P2716.**

[The following is an extract from a poem intended to censure a woman identified as the mother of Ahmad Sahyoon]

> My vagina was reared in disobedience
> With elderly men and young boys
> And grinding is a permanent fixture
> They call me the mother of malice
> And among scandals I came to be.
> If I was thrown in fire
> Then by my magic it would disappear.
>
> I am the old hag, the mother of riding
> Between an elephant and a mule
> And I drive them without halter or leash.
> In grinding I came to know vaginas
> And in sodomy a target is my rear.

ENDNOTES

[1] This lecture was delivered on February 3, 2008, at the Feminist Coalition Complex in Haifa. It was originally written and delivered in Arabic. The Arabic transcript of this lecture was published by Aswat in 2008 under the title *al-Mithliya al-Jinsiya fil Sharq al-Awsat: Tarikhuha wa Taswiruha* and can also be accessed electronically at http://www.aswatgroup.org/FileServer/da6578 849b3b6e92869204b68f96c036.pdf last accessed February 26, 2009.

[2] The delivery of this lecture coincided with the launch of Aswat's second Arabic-language book. *My Right to Live, to Choose, to Be: A Collection of Literary Texts Written by Arab Lesbian Women* is an anthology of creative works. Aswat's previous book contains both original and translated feminist and queer research in Arabic. *Home and Exile in Queer Experience Collection of Articles about Lesbian and Homosexual Identity* was published by Aswat in 2006.

[3] I also noticed that there is a connection between the cautionary tale of qawm Lut as told in the Quran and the other cautionary tale about qawm Thamoud. Qawm Thamoud were annihilated by Allah, also due to their disbelief, and their rejection of the prophet Saleh. This is very similar to the cautionary tale regarding qawm Lut who were also annihilated for disbelief and in addition, seeking to rape an angel.

[4] Bathal was a skilled musician and singer who was renowned for her talent in the court of al-Ma'mun at the time.

⁵ Original word *nafeer*, which is a "musical" instrument that is used in gathering or collecting the people of a village or an army regiment.

⁶ In communication with Fadia Abboud via email, January 27, 2008.

⁷ Ibid.

⁸ I refer to chapters in part II of my monograph, *Female Homosexuality in the Middle East: Histories and Representations* (New York and London: Routledge, 2007), 47-83.

⁹ Alison Eves, "Queer Theory, Butch/Femme Identities and Lesbian Space" (*Sexualities* 7.4, 2004), 481.

¹⁰ Ironically and significantly, I was not able to find a single reference to harem lesbian activities in any of the medieval Arabic texts I perused.

¹¹ This view is not exclusive to western narratives of female homosexuality in the Arab world, but is rather begotten from the view propounded by the homophobic or misguided rhetoric of certain Arab scholars and critics themselves. In the medieval period, it was understood that *some* women were more interested in avoiding pregnancy and scandal and hence resorted to sexual relations with other women; however, this was not seen as the predominant trait or "reason" for most grinders (as it came to be known in the modern period).

¹² The original word is *Fayashil* which refers to the stimulation of the clitoris with the tip of the penis.

[13] This poem is cited by Tifashi [d. 1253]. Its origin is uncertain; it could be from any period prior to the thirteenth century.

[14] This is the medieval name granted to women who engage in sexual activities with other women.

[15] See *Female Homosexuality in the Middle East*, 52-53.

[16] Eves, 481-482.

[17] In particular, I refer to the works of David Halperin: *One Hundred Years of Homosexuality: and other essays on Greek love* (New York: Routledge, 1989); and Halperin et al., eds., *Before Sexuality: The Construction of Erotic Experience in the Ancient Greek World* (Princeton: Princeton University Press, 1990). Craig A. Williams takes an approach similar to Halperin's in *Roman Homosexuality: Ideologies of Masculinity in Classical Antiquity* (Oxford: Oxford University Press, 1999).

[18] Michel Foucault, *The Use of Pleasure: The History of Sexuality* vol.2, trans. Robert Hurley ([Paris, 1984], London: Penguin, 1992), 3.

[19] As Nietzsche famously indicated, "The 'thing itself' (for that is what pure truth, without consequences, would be) is quite incomprehensible to the creators of language and not at all worth aiming for." See Friedrich Nietzsche, "On Truth and Lies in an Extra-Moral Sense" [1873], in Walter Kaufman, trans. and ed., *Portable Nietzsche* (London: Chatto and Windus, 1971), 45.

[20] Irshad Manji, *The Trouble with Islam: A Muslim's Call for Reform in Her Faith*. (Sydney: Random House, 2003), 143.

²¹ Richard Burton, trans., "Tale of Kamar al-Zaman" in *The Arabian Nights*, vol. 3 ([Iran]: printed by Burton Club, [c.1888]), 303.

²² There have been numerous studies that discuss the figure of the tribade. For a treatment of the particular issue of hypertrophied clitorises and its relation to the intersexed body, see Theresa Braunschneider, "The Macroclitoride, the Tribade and the Woman: Configuring Gender and Sexuality in English Anatomical Discourse" (*Textual Practice* 13.3, 1999), 509-532.

²³ I particularly admire the meta-historical theoretical framework in Sarah Toulalan's "Extraordinary Satisfactions: Lesbian Visibility in Seventeenth-Century Pornography in England" (*Gender and History* 15.1, 2003), 50-68, and Susan Lanser's "'Au sein de vos pareilles': Sapphic Separatism in Late Eighteenth-Century France" (*Journal of Homosexuality* 41.3/4, 2001), 105-116.

²⁴ أشير هنا إلى الجزء II من دراستي "المثلية الجنسية عند النساء في الشرق الأوسط: تاريخ وتصوير". نيويورك ولندن: روتلدج، 2007. 83.47

²⁵ أليسون إيف. "نظرية تحرير الجنس ، هويات النساء ومساحة السحاقية". في الجنس. 7 (4) ، 2004.481

²⁶ في الحقيقة، تهكّماً ودلالة، لم أجد مرجعاً واحداً للنشاطات السحقية في الحريم في أيّ من النصوص العربية في القرون الوسطى، التي قرأتها.

²⁷ هذه الصورة غير محصورة بالكتاب الغربيين الذين تناولوا في كتاباتهم موضوع المثلية الجنسية عند النساء في العالم العربي، ولكنها انبثقت من صورة تمّ اقتراحها في نص نثري مثلي أو مضلّل لأحد علماء العرب والناقدين. في مرحلة القرون الوسطى، كان من الطبيعي أن يلجأ بعض النساء إلى إقامة علاقات جنسية مع نساء أخريات لتفادي الوقوع في الحمل والفضيحة، غير أنّ ذلك لم يكن السبب الطاغي للذهاب إلى السحق كما أصبح شائعاً في الفترة المعاصرة.

²⁸ الكلمة الأصل هي فياشل أي إثارة البظر بواسطة طرف القضيب.

²⁹ هذا الشعر لتيفاشي د.1253. مصدره غير أكيد ويمكن أنّ يعود لأي فترة من الفترات التي سبقت القرن الثالث عشر.

³⁰ هو الإسم الذي أطلق على النساء في القرون الوسطى اللواتي كنّ يمارسن نشاطات جنسية مع أخريات.

31 العودة إلى "المثلية الجنسية عند النساء في الشرق الأوسط"، 52-53.

32 أشير بشكل خاص إلى أعمال دايفد هالبيرين "مائة عام من المثلية" وبعض الكتابات الأخرى التي تتناول موضوع الحبّ الإغريقي. نيويورك: راوتلدج، 1989؛ وهالبرين و.al.Eds قبل الجنس: تكوّن الخبرة الشهوانية في عالم الإغريق القديم. برينستون: صحيفة جامعة برينستون، 1990. قارب كريغ أ. وليامز بشكل مشابه لأسلوب هالبيرين المثلية الجنسية عند الإغريق: أيديولوجيات الذكورية في العصور القديمة. أكسفورد: صحيفة جامعة أكسفورد، 1999.

33 كما كتب نيتشي: ""الموضوع بحدّ ذاته" (وهي الحقيقة الصرف/ من دون أي نتائج أبداً) هو موضوع صعب فهمه بالنسبة إلى مبدعي اللغة ولا يستحقّ أبداً التطلّع إليه." العودة إلى فريدريك نيتشي" عن الحقيقة والكذب في حسّ أخلاقي". [1873] . ترجمة وتدقيق والتر كوفمان.

34 إرشاد منجي، المشكلة مع الإسلام: نداء مسلمة لإصلاح إيمانها"، سيدني، راندم هاوس، 2003. 143.

35 ريتشارد بورتن، ترجمة "حكاية قمر الزمان" في اليالي الحمراء، الجزء 3، [إيران]: تمّ الطبع من قبل نادي بورتن، [c 1888]، 303

36 دراسات عدّة تناقش موضوع شكل المتذكرة. من أجل معالجة موضوع البظور المتضخّمة وعلاقتها بالجسم المزدوج الجنسية، العودة إلى تيريزا براونشنايدر. "ضخامة البظر، tribadism والمرأة: تصوير الجنس والجنسية في سياق إنكليزي تشريحي". التطبيق النصي" 13(3) 1999 :509-532.

37 Nous faisons référence aux chapitres de la partie II de notre monographie paru dans *Homosexualité des femmes au Moyen Orient : Histoires et représentations*. New York & Londres: Routledge, 2007 : 47-83.

38 Alison Eves. "Théorie de l'homosexualité, /identités de femme / hommasse et espace lesbien." *Sexualities*. 7(4), 2004 : 481.

39 Il est à la fois ironique et significatif que nous n'ayons pu trouver une seule référence aux activités des lesbiennes de harem dans les textes arabes de la période médiévale que nous avons parcouru.

⁴⁰ Ce point de vue n'est pas exclusive aux narrations occidentales de l'homosexualité des femmes dans le monde arabe, mais provient plutôt du point de vue de la rhétorique homophobe ou maladroite de certains chercheurs et critiques arabes. Pendant la période médiévale, il était admis que *certaines* femmes étaient plus intéressées à éviter de tomber enceintes et de causer un scandale. Elles faisaient donc recours aux rapports sexuels avec d'autres femmes. Cependant, cela n'était pas considéré comme la caractéristique ou la « raison » la plus importante pour la plupart des copulatrices, comme ce fut le cas pendant la période moderne.

⁴¹ Le terme original est *Fayashil* et fait référence à la stimulation du clitoris avec le bout du pénis.

⁴² Ce poème est cite par Tifashi d. 1253. Son origine est incertaine et il pourrait dater d'avant le treizième siècle.

⁴³ C'est le nom médiéval donné aux femmes qui ont des rapports sexuels avec d'autres femmes.

⁴⁴ Voir *Homosexualité des femmes au Moyen Orient*, 52-53.

⁴⁵ Nous faisons particulièrement référence aux travaux de David Halperin *Cent ans d'homosexualité : et autres essais sur l'amour en Grèce*. New York: Routledge, 1989; et Halperin *et al.* (Eds). *Avant la sexualité : La construction de l'expérience érotique dans la Grèce antique*. Princeton: Princeton University Press, 1990. Craig A. Williams adopte une approche similaire à celle de Halperin dans *Homosexualité romaine : Idéologies de la masculinité dans l'Antiquité*. Oxford: Oxford University Press, 1999.

⁴⁶ Comme Nietzsche l'a si bien dit : "La "chose elle-même" (parce que c'est cela la pure vérité, sans conséquences) est assez incompréhensible aux créateurs de la langue et ne vaut pas du tout la peine d'être recherchée." Voir Fredrich Nietzsche *Introduction théorétique sur la vérité et le mensonge au sens extra-moral*" [1873]. Traduit et édité. Walter Kaufman. *Le Nietzsche de poche.* Londres : Chatto & Windus, 1971. 45.

⁴⁷ Irshad Manji, *Musulmane, mais libre.* Sydney: Random House, 2003. 143.

⁴⁸ Richard Burton, trad. "Conte de Kamar al-Zaman" dans *Les Nuits d'Arabie*, vol. 3, ([Iran]: Imprimé par Burton Club, [c.1888]), 303.

⁴⁹ Il y a eu plusieurs études qui parlent de la silhouette de la tribade. Pour une discussion de cette question particulière des clitoris hypertrophiés et de son rapport au corps intersexué, voir Theresa Braunschneider. "The Macroclitoride, the Tribade and the Woman: Configuring Gender and Sexuality in English Anatomical Discourse." *Textual Practice* 13(3) 1999: 509-532.

⁵⁰ Nous avons une admiration particulière pour le cadre théorique méta-historique dans "Extraordinary Satisfactions: Lesbian Visibility in Seventeenth-Century Pornography in England." de Sarah Toulalan dans *Gender and History* 15(1) avril 2003 : 50-68 et "'Au sein de vos pareilles': Sapphic Separatism in Late Eighteenth-Century France." de Susan Lanser dans *Journal of Homosexuality* 41(3/4) 2001: 105-116.

⁵¹ That is, she is able to relax and let the man "do the work" (raha).

[52] *Fataroo*: If a man gets an erection (simply by looking) during the month of Ramadan, during daylight, then it is said that he has broken his fast.

[53] Original word *Lutiyeen*, referring to the people of Lot.

[54] Bathal was a skilled musician and singer who was renowned for her talent in the court of Al-Ma'mun at the time.

[55] A woman's *Mahram* is a male relation such as her father, uncle, brother, cousin and also husband. In this instance, the woman is forbidden to make her skin (except face and hands) visible except to these men. In some Islamic cultures, past and present, women are not permitted to travel on their own or without the company of a *Mahram*.

[56] *Mubashara*: more closely resembles the concept of foreplay than embracing, and may involve nudity.

[57] Taher Haddad's compilation of the Arabic text relies on Gotha manuscript # 2045 and Berlin # 6381.

[58] *Fatat*—an adolescent, not a child and not quite a woman.

[59] As opposed to being a beloved.

[60] *Mukaree'at*: women who read the Quran by singing it.

[61] The term *sahq*, which is best translated as "grinding" refers specifically to female-to-female eroticism primarily focused on the clitoris, which, it is clear from the text, was neither properly investigated in the medical discourse of the time nor properly discovered. Later we learn, from Tifashi himself, the specific

mode of clitoral stimulation undertaken by the grinders. The text suggests that there were no other modes for clitoral stimulation or same-sex sexual practices, which is perhaps more of an indication of the limited resources available to Tifashi than the cultural truth the text aims to reflect.

[62] *Melilotus Indicus*.

[63] i.e. adopted, chosen.

[64] Fedwa Malti Douglas translates grinding as tribadism, which is a particularly accurate description here. See Fedwa Malti Douglas, "Tribadism/Lesbianism and the Sexualised Body in Medieval Arabo-Islamic Narrative" in Francesca Canadé Sautman and Pamela Sheingorn, eds., *Same Sex Love and Desire Among Women in the Middle Ages* (New York: Palgrave, 2001), 123-141. Note that the first time Tifashi refers to wise men, they appear to be speaking or analysing in favour of homosexual grinders. Later when he reveals to us his own experience and encounters in the matter, we find him offering such superlative descriptions of the women's cleanliness and highly stylised tastes.

[65] The original word used is *Tharaf*.

[66] This is the same word—device—that appears as a euphemistic term for the penis in the beginning of the chapter.

[67] The word originally used in one of the manuscripts is *jawzatan* which can also mean, or at least can have the connotations of, "two wives." The editor of the modern Arabic edition, Jamal Juma'a informs us that the word was then replaced by "the two women" (238).

[68] i.e. from the city.

[69] Alternatively this could be translated as "And the one below was making only very few replies, as though she was a student of hers."

[70] Presumably here, the judge is wearing a banner or flag that would distinguish his social standing. It may have been tied to each of his shins with cords, or across his torso.

[71] Original word *Thuwuul* which is plural for tail or appendix.

[72] A peculiar way of saying that he does not wish to have sex with her.

[73] Original word *nafeer*, which is a "musical" instrument that is used in summoning the people of a village or an army regiment.

[74] The original word is *Fayashil* which refers to the stimulation of the clitoris with the tip of the penis.

[75] Primary use for a stick: to guide you in darkness, also a reference to poor execution of the sexual act.

[76] Originally *Waras* which refers to the part of the Saffron plant (Crocus Sativus) that is yellow in colour; the stigma which is also known as the pistil is the female reproductive organ of the plant.

[77] Exposed in a scandalous manner.

[78] *Suhoor*: A time before daylight where the faster, especially during the month of Ramadan, can eat her/his last meal before abstinence from food throughout the daylight. The faithful also abstain from sexual thoughts and activity during the light of day.

An erection, for a man, during daylight in the month of Ramadan, constitutes breaking the fast.

[79] The original word is *Thawat* which may mean "dignitaries" or simply "those in possession of." Since the word has such an interesting connotation, contrary to the reprimanding tone of the poem, I thought it fit to preserve the contradiction.

[80] i.e. food filling eaten with bread.

[81] i.e. handle.

[82] The sounds of these names, which are in themselves references to figures in the Judeo-Christian-Muslim theological tradition, also connote the phonetics of the Arabic words for "grinding" and "penis" respectively.

[83] Can also be read: Women can only have sex with each other if they are fornicators.

www.ingramcontent.com/pod-product-compliance
Lightning Source LLC
Chambersburg PA
CBHW070921180426
43192CB00038B/2103